À bientôt …

Also by Roger Moore

My Word is My Bond

Bond on Bond

Last Man Standing

À bientôt ...

ROGER MOORE

with Gareth Owen

Michael O'Mara Books Limited

First published in Great Britain in 2017 by
Michael O'Mara Books Limited
9 Lion Yard
Tremadoc Road
London SW4 7NQ

A CIP catalogue record for this book is available from the British
Library.

Papers used by Michael O'Mara Books Limited are natural,
recyclable products made from wood grown in sustainable forests.
The manufacturing processes conform to the environmental
regulations of the country of origin.

ISBN: 978-1-78243-861-8 in hardback print format
ISBN: 978-1-78243-862-5 in ebook format

1 2 3 4 5 6 7 8 9 10

Designed and typeset by Ana Bjezancevic
Illustrations from the author's private collection unless credited
otherwise

Printed and bound by CPI Group (UK) Ltd, Croydon, CR0 4YY

www.mombooks.com

CONTENTS

FOREWORD

by DEBORAH MOORE

Not so long ago Dad and I were having a laugh about the pros and cons of getting older. He was complaining, which he seldom did, about his knees and the tingling he would get in his feet that would drive him mad. Those two 'cons' of old age he managed because of his unbelievable zest for life and the totally optimistic approach he had to everything.

'I still feel as if I am in my twenties,' he told me. 'But when I look in the mirror I say, "Who the hell are you?!"'

My father was not a vain man in the least and his childlike sense of humour meant that he embraced getting older with such dignity and fortitude.

For Dad, the 'pros' of getting older were seeing his grandchildren grow and spending time with his family, for whom he had so much love and time to give.

He was, as he himself would be the first to admit, somewhat of a hypochondriac: chemists were to him what Jimmy Choo is to those daft enough to love walking in high heels. My apologies, ladies!

He always had the best doctors and so, when he became ill just after Christmas 2016 and having embarked on writing this book, he never for a minute thought that he would not live to see it published.

With the help of his trustworthy and favourite co-star/ PA Gareth Owen, he did finish this book of memories and funny incidents he experienced throughout his life and I hope that you the reader will laugh with and at the antics that my beloved Dad got up to − and away with.

I am sure he is telling his naughty jokes to all his mates up in the heavens and giving the angels something to flutter their wings about.

I love you, Dad.

Deborah

INTRODUCTION

The poet Dante believed old age starts at forty-five. The United Nations suggests it begins at sixty. Meanwhile, in 2016, the *Daily Express* newspaper reported that Britons do not see themselves as elderly until they are nudging eighty-five.

Well, as I write, I'm in my ninetieth year. Ninety! Where did those years go?

But what is 'old age'? Does it define us? Does it inhibit us? You can't escape it, you can't avoid it – well, you can, but the alternative isn't to be recommended – so you just have to embrace it. Mind you, 'Old Folks' Home' doesn't exactly sound like a place you want to add to your bucket list, does it? It has a ring of finality about it, and that's why the graceful Dame Judi Dench says she doesn't allow the word 'old' to be spoken in her house, as it suggests she is past it – and that is quite clearly not the case.

Do I feel old? Not at all! Though my body may creak and groan a bit more now than it used to.

It always amuses me that children measure their years in fractions: 'I'm three and a quarter' or 'I'm four and a half!', before rounding it *up* as soon as possible. Later on in life, you'll find people do the reverse, insisting that they're not almost ninety-five, but ninety-four-and-three-quarters. Better still, in middle age, we don't use fractions; we use euphemisms such as 'fifty-plus' or the 'third age'. While children and teenagers long to grow older and acquire the greater freedoms and privileges that come with ageing – it used to be your twenty-first birthday but now it's your eighteenth – the cosmetics industry and the anti-ageing market has extended at both ends, with endless products and potions for 'mature' skin, but also anti-ageing creams for twenty-somethings …

When my publishers reminded me I am going to be fairly ancient this year, they suggested I might once again put finger to keyboard and come up with a tome to tie in with my upcoming celebration. I started reflecting and thinking about age, people, places and the good fortune I've enjoyed across these past decades. This is a book about some of those memories, many irreverent, along with some thoughts of what might have been, some sideways glances, and a few grumbles. You see I've lived through so many landmark events – ranging from the introduction of television, World War II, the first man on the moon, the start and end of the Cold War, the birth of the internet ... and so very much more. I suddenly realized that yes, I really am that old.

Then, there are some of the absurdities advancing age brings with it. For example:

- When you still feel twenty-one inside but wonder who the old fart in the bathroom mirror staring back at you is.

- When you thought 'sick' meant someone was ill.

- When you tune into the radio and hear they're playing 'a golden oldie', only to realize it's from 1988.

- When you realize 'easy-open tin' is the very definition of an oxymoron.

- When you look at a bathtub and wonder, if you get in it, will you ever get out?

With my tongue firmly placed in my cheek, it's now time to get on …

With my older cousin Doreen who liked to keep me firmly grounded with tales of our youth together.

A SENSE OF
NINETY YEARS

When contemplating how to start this book I thought I would cast my mind back to my earliest memories, which is not as easy as you might think. It was then that I realized that so many recollections are not in fact linked to places or dates, but rather to smells and sounds. I shouldn't be too surprised I guess, as, after all, we humans have five main senses: sight, touch, taste, plus the all-important smell and hearing. Yet rarely do we appreciate just how intrinsically those last two are linked to our most treasured memories.

Whenever I picture my parents I instantly get a waft of my mother's favourite perfume and my father's trusted aftershave lotion. These fragrances are etched onto my brain and, along with other childhood smells, hold a privileged status in my memory bank, conjuring up all sorts of happy thoughts. Some experts say that smells trigger memories because our ancestors were more dependent on their noses to avoid poisonous plants, rotten food or enemies about to attack … I prefer to think they just evoke happy memories!

I still feel very comforted whenever I think of my parents. They were there throughout my formative years, teaching me, guiding me, caring for me and loving me. Whenever I drift back in thought to the family flat in 1930s Stockwell, south London, I can clearly picture my mother in the kitchen – she was always cooking something tasty. Now, the merest sniff of cooking apples takes me right back to standing at her side as she opened the oven door and produced a golden-brown apple pie. Despite having consumed hundreds, if not thousands, of apple pies over the years, not one ever tasted as good as Mum's, especially if she added a dollop of cream or a glug of Bird's custard over the top. If ever I catch sight of a food programme on TV and steak and kidney pudding is mentioned, I'm right back there in the kitchen, watching Mum mixing the ingredients for her pastry. Like the Bisto Kid, my nose would cock and sniff the air when I arrived home from school and, I hoped, might report back that there was a rice pudding, or a sponge cake, or perhaps raspberry-flavoured blancmange being prepared – and if I was lucky I'd be able to lick the bowl! That was the best bit, and what a treat. One thing is for sure, no restaurant could ever conjure up a home-cooked meal that tastes as good.

Mum's apple pie, seldom bettered but often improved with a dollop of custard.

The smell of Mum's food staying with me betrays my greedy streak – I can quite often make a pig of myself with comfort foods. Meat and two veg, sometimes three if we were flush, was the typical and staple diet of my formative years. Mind you, it wasn't all Delia Smith. The aroma of boiling cabbage was pretty dreadful, but the smell I loathed most was the fish heads being boiled up for the cat's dinner.

That smell lingered around the flat for days and was the most unpleasant, if not rotten, thing your airways could possibly encounter.

On the other hand, carbolic − or coal tar − soap which many people say smells like leather, is hugely nostalgic and pleasing to me. I was obviously an odd child who rather liked the bleached, antiseptic smell of doctors' surgeries and hospital corridors and carbolic was what you might call the 'signature smell' of such places. It was very effective, and many was the bath night when I had a good scrub with a bar of it to eliminate all dirt marks, bugs and germs.

Consequently, I'd like to think I was a very clean child, who dutifully always washed behind his ears − when being watched, at

Did you MACLEAN your teeth today?

"Yes, they've so healthy"

MACLEANS
Peroxide Tooth Paste
makes teeth
WHITER

An early ad – once again, cleanliness was my watchword!

least – though imagine the horror when Nitty Nora used to descend on our school to examine our hair for head lice. I'm sure she was a very kindly person in real life, though her bedside – or deskside – manner left a bit to be desired as she roughly rifled through our follicles before dispatching any diseased boys and girls home with a note: 'Your child has hair lice.'

You can't help getting older, but you don't have to get old …

GEORGE BURNS

My mother would reassure me by saying that the lice only liked living on clean heads, before producing a bar of what I think was some sort of foul-smelling paraffin-based soap, whipping it into a lather and smothering it all over my hair, leaving it on overnight to form a sort of crusty, sticky mound. (I'm really selling this to you, aren't I?) Next morning, it could be brushed out with a special comb, and more than a little force, the hope being that it enshrined all the trapped lice in its plaster-like texture.

WHAT IF ...?

Percy Shelley (1961)

Back in 1961 a cutting from the *Evening Standard* from 24 July stated, '[Roger Moore] having given up TV and taken on the status of an independent actor, is anxious to do more serious things. He is proposing to appear in a film of the life of the poet Shelley.' Needless to say the idea of me becoming a serious actor convinced no one, and playing a major English romantic poet was maybe stretching my range. It fell to the BBC a decade later to make a TV film with Robert Powell in the lead.

As a child I spent a lot of time at the cinema, and cinemas also had a peculiar smell all of their own – usually featuring a mixture of stale cigarette smoke, mixed with a whiff of damp and a bit of orange peel. Those were the days when you'd see the projection beam mid-air between the box and the screen because of the huge amount of smoke rising in the auditorium, tarnishing the walls and ceiling with a disgusting brown nicotine. But did we care? Certainly not!

Saturday mornings and the 'Tuppenny Rush' were magical times for me and my pals, passive smoking or not!

In the streets, you could always smell fresh bread coming from the door of our local bakers on the corner, who had to change their German name, Aichroth, to the more Scottish-sounding Kerr at the outbreak of war. On some Saturday mornings they offered me the chance of helping them out, carrying the trays of buns and bread, for the reward of as many buns as I could eat. The butcher's shop had a completely different appearance and smell, of course: raw meat mixed with the sweet smell of the sawdust on the tiled floor to help absorb the blood and fat and stop people from slipping over.

Monday was always washday, and you'd hear washtubs bubbling away, mangles creaking and then a dazzling display of white hanging from washing lines as proud housewives showed what good, clean houses they were running. If it was raining, wooden clothes horses would be stood indoors, next to the fire, to dry the clothes while giving off a whiff of damp. You'd also hear the whirring grind of the mincer machine on Mondays, as any meat left over from the Sunday joint would be minced up to make another meal, perhaps with some bubble and squeak plopped on top, all fried up with a knob of lard.

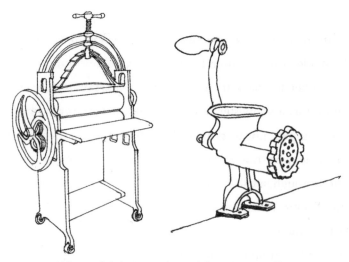

Where did the mangle and the mincer go?

I've always loved swimming and aside from the local baths and lido, as teenagers my mates and I used to head up to swim in the Thames around Richmond. It always seemed clear, clean and fresh there – ah, that lovely fresh water smell. The river's posher at that end, so perhaps it was less dirty, though you still wouldn't want to swallow too much of it and risk getting an upset stomach. I know they've cleaned the Thames up in recent decades, but when David Walliams did his 140-mile charity swim in the river in 2011, I did wonder if he might suffer any side effects from ingesting the odd mouthful. When we met he told me that 'Thames Tummy' had given him diarrhoea, vomiting and low energy levels. Perhaps it's still not quite *that* clean?

In ancient times, river water was so contaminated that the staple drink was beer. I don't know whether I was around in another life back then, but one of the stranger things I enjoyed as a youngster was visiting a pub first thing in the morning. No, not to get a drink but rather because I had an uncle who ran a pub in the village of Ramsey, near Peterborough, a village of two streets, a post office and about fifteen pubs. Whenever I stayed there, I would join my uncle early in the morning as he went downstairs into the bar: as soon as he pushed the door open, the smell of beer-soaked wood, polish and old shag tobacco would hit my nostrils. There was something oddly comforting and homely about it.

I was a strange child at times.

School had drinking fountains, though under no circumstances should you drink the water in the toilets. Well, no, not the toilet itself, but from the washbasin taps. Yet again, thinking of a particular thing brings back the smells of polished parquet floors, carbolic-saturated corridors with the odd whiff of glue and paint from the art rooms mixed in, and, finally, the highly bleached toilets. Why do I persist in turning my mind to the smallest room? For the very simple reason that my mind is etched with the memory of the glossy toilet paper in the cubicles, which was more like tracing paper. Quite what absorption properties or benefits

21

it offered remain a mystery to me, but I do know it likely contributed to many cases of haemorrhoids in later life.

I was always told not to drink too much before bedtime. It was a lesson I heeded while touring in my early career, as quite often the only bathroom would be down several flights of stairs or, heaven forbid, down the garden path.

During my time in the forces – not in the war but just after, during the two years of National Service – my first six weeks of basic training were spent in Bury St Edmunds. There, thirty young recruits were housed in a hut with fifteen bunk beds. National Service was compulsory and all young men were, sooner or later, obliged to enrol, whether they wanted to or not. I soon learned, as a willing soldier, that you should always try to get the top bunk because if there was somebody less willing, they would inevitably try to 'work their ticket', that is to say, get a medical discharge, and the favoured way of achieving the first step in a discharge was by proving you'd lost control of your bladder. Many was the time those on the lower bunks woke up to the delights of a urine-soaked blanket.

Later, when I was working as an actor on foreign film locations, we were often warned about drinking the water, and told that bottled water was the only option. Well, in principle, that's all well and good but you'd always find that

22

With a pal in Copenhagen during National Service.

the local caterers would wash the salad and make ice cubes from the said undrinkable H_2O.

I often wished I had the constitution of John Huston and Humphrey Bogart, who only ever drank whisky when they were on location in the deepest darkest jungles on *The African Queen* (1951). All the crew fell ill with awful waterborne bugs and parasites, all bar the director and star who seemed immune.

It often amuses me when visitors to our chalet in Switzerland ask, 'Is the water OK to drink here?'

'Just down the hill, they're bottling and selling it all around the world,' I reply.

Buses, underground trains and trams have their own distinct aroma. It's partly pollution, I now realize, but the unique blend of fumes, dust, engine oil, tarmac and cast iron all hit you as a train coming in to a platform pushes all the blended smells in front of it, in a warmed-up wall of air, usually coupled with the 'singing' noise that the train makes on the tracks as it approaches – totally unique. I recently read that, today, the pollution underground is eight times greater than above ground – and people breath it in!

In my formative years we had coal-powered steam trains, and the soot they pushed out was phenomenal. What with them and all the factory chimneys bellowing out smoke, it's no wonder London was often under a smog.

When I started on *The Saint* in 1962 I remember the smogs that were still hanging over London and its suburbs, and in the film studios the shop steward would shout 'Travellers away!' so the crew who had a distance to get home could leave before it set in thick. I think the worst case was a decade earlier, in December 1952, when a real pea-souper descended, quite unprecedented, and lasted four or five days due to a mix of pollutants and a cold, windless weather spell. It was reported that up to 12,000 people died.

❧

We don't grow older, we grow riper.
PABLO PICASSO

❧

Thankfully, steam engines were increasingly being replaced by diesel, and while not hugely less polluting they did have the effect of pumping out somewhat less fumes and we saw fewer smogs as a result.

I don't know if it's a child thing or a male thing, but I was fascinated by steam trains and would stand for hours on a railway bridge looking for a train coming, and as it went under the bridge I'd rush across to the other side to see the smoke emerge again. A curious sound, which you wouldn't encounter near railway lines these days, were the loud explosions, similar to a shotgun going off. The railway companies actually set detonators in the form of large percussion caps on the rails, which were activated by the wheels of an oncoming train to provide an audible warning to match the signal indicators, in case the driver couldn't see them in the fog.

While we're on the subject of smells, I'll be perfectly frank with you and say I've never quite understood how

25

some people don't seem to notice their own body odour. Forgive me, but when you've been on as many film locations as me, you get to know which members of the crew to give a wide berth to – and it's usually the ones who wear shorts, white socks and sandals. They permeate the air with quite the foulest fragrance, backed up with the visual assurance of wet armpits and T-shirts stuck to their backs. It's not the sweat that smells, of course, but the bacteria on the skin that breaks down as a result and stinks just like a rotting cheese. Break out the carbolic, say I! Remote film locations are not always the easiest places to get a shower or bath, I know, but when you're filming a block away from a plush hotel, there's really no excuse.

Of course, I was always brought up to believe ladies don't sweat or perspire, and was told they simply 'glow'. Well, I feel I can admit this now: I've been stuck in elevators with a few glowing ladies in my time and, let me tell you, there's nothing very pleasant about it or them!

We can't leave smells without mentioning the elephant in the room … what we might call the 'rear activity'. An explosion from the rear quarters. A fart. Trumping. Tooting. Passing gas. Breaking wind or gas. As one gets older one finds one (note I didn't use 'I' here – heaven forbid that anyone should think these things happen to me!) has less control over when they are expelled and the nature of said explosion. Strange as it may seem, both Leslie Nielsen and Cary Grant were quite fascinated by farts; Leslie even had a little hand-held fart machine that he'd take with him everywhere. It was a tiny machine he concealed in the palm of his hand and quite often, mid-conversation on a chat show, he would innocently 'let one off'. He had a wonderful ability to keep a totally straight face in its wake. He also revelled in using it in packed elevators, and at dinner parties when he was introduced or was chatting with total strangers you could guarantee he'd press the button. There was great comedy in watching other people's reactions to Leslie's nonplussed expression. He was asked to leave restaurants on several occasions, and was even moved to window seats aboard aircrafts for letting one off every time someone walked past his aisle seat. He was a one-man flatulence factory.

Long before music streaming was ever thought of, and CDs had replaced vinyl, our only real source of music and the spoken word was the radio or wireless, which was the constant sound in the background throughout my childhood. Our set was almost always tuned to the BBC Light Programme,

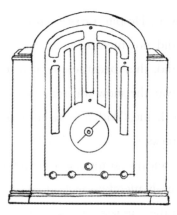

Radio was a huge influence in our lives – in every way.

the entertainment channel, the only other station being the Home Service, which was more news-based. It's funny but all these years on, I can still instantly recognize the music to certain shows, such as the comedy *It's That Man Again* (*ITMA*), and *Music While You Work*, which broadcast very lively music with a rapid beat. As a youngster I just loved hearing all the popular tunes and it wasn't until much later that I found out that the broadcast was designed to encourage the women working in the factories to speed up production.

Sunday lunchtime brought *Forces Favourites* with Jean Metcalfe and her co-presenter, Squadron Leader Cliff Michelmore, who was based in Hamburg (and he used the very same Officers' Mess that I did when I was later stationed there with the Combined Services Entertainment

Unit after the war). Despite broadcasting together weekly, Jean and Cliff did not meet face to face for six months, but when they did, they became engaged and married in 1950. After the war, the show was renamed *Two-Way Family Favourites*, and its theme, 'With a Song in My Heart', can still stop me in my tracks.

If I were to tell my grandchildren today that when I was a child all family members came together in one room, huddled around the wireless set, with the coal fire banked up in the background, waiting patiently for the valves to warm up and for the wireless to spring, or rather limp, into life while we all stared at it, despite its lack of pictures – they'd probably think I was mad.

The radio was sometimes overshadowed by my father picking the strings of his banjo or ukulele and the one piece he played over and over again was 'Whispering' by Paul Whiteman. Another favourite was 'Over the Waves', a classic melody from fairgrounds and circuses that is one of those tunes you just 'know' without actually knowing what it's called or who wrote it. I smiled widely when it later turned up in *The Great Caruso* (1951) movie, and my favourite scene was when Mrs Caruso (Ann Blyth), about to reveal to her husband that she was pregnant, was waltzing with him to that very tune and then starts to sing.

'I did not know you could sing,' says Caruso.

'Every mother should know a lullaby,' she replies.

What a moment!

We got most of our news from newspapers and the wireless, of course, but our dose of visual news footage was supplied by a visit to the cinema to see the Pathé Newsreel – which reported things days, if not weeks, after they happened. There was no live link-up by satellite; no twenty-four-hour rolling news. However, there was always a mad dash to leave at the end of the programme – which in addition to the newsreel also contained a short or supporting film, along with the main feature – as the national anthem was always played, and nobody really wanted to stand rigid waiting for it to end, nor risk missing the bus home.

There are so many sounds around towns and cities that you never hear any more. 'Any old iron, any old iron?' from the rag and bone men, trotting around on their horses and carts collecting old clothes, scrap metal and just about anything else people were going to otherwise throw away. You'd often find a trail of horse dung left behind, as with the drayman and coalman's carts too, which, if you were enterprising, you could shovel up and sell for a few pennies down at the local allotments.

Then there was the call of the bread man in his little

van, the milkman with his cry of 'milko, milko' and even the chimes of the ice cream van – I know they still exist, but they're not as prolific as they were in my youth, when you used to see them on every street corner. Occasionally the 'knife man' would appear on the street in his van, and you'd hear a grinding noise and maybe even see the odd spark coming from the back of the van as he sharpened carving knives, clippers, shears and just about anything else housewives would present.

Every road in London seemed to have nightly works going on, and on every corner there would be night watchman standing guard, usually with a coke brazier. We children would take along a potato and ask him to bake it

Another early advert. 'They're delicious, they're irresistible, they melt hearts ...' The chocolates, not me.

for us in the red flames, and the taste − delicious! − was almost as good as the comforting, warm aroma.

In later life the sound I loved best was that of applause for a young aspiring actor walking out on stage. Standing in the wings, just before the curtain goes up, you wait for the audience to hush then take the brave steps out. Oh, the anticipation on their expectant faces! Mind you, it was swiftly followed by the great disappointment of seeing me!

Although film studios didn't have audiences, they did have appreciative crews who were sometimes kind enough to offer a round of applause when I got through a scene without fluffing the script. Unique to stages in studios the world over is the smell of dust, paint and burning filters on lamps that often went 'pop', blowing a bulb at a crucial moment!

Though phased out by the early 1970s, the 'three-strip' Technicolor cameras, which arguably offered the very best colour, were huge custom-made machines that actually ran three separate strips of film through them at the same time. The camera was so noisy that it required a huge 'blimp' of soundproof housing and the actual camera, plus the blimp, weighed a ton. Imagine trying to get one of those into a car to film a driving sequence?

The first sight of the young Ivanhoe.

WARTIME MEMORIES

Which war you ask? Well, I may be old but I'm not referring to the bloody Boer War, that's for sure! World War II (1939–45), or (1942–1945 for American readers), dominated my teenage years and so plays a big part in my early memories. So very many things happened, yet oddly, what springs to my mind was the great outbreak of impetigo that afflicted many children at that time, along with a scabies epidemic. With these skin infections you'd come up in rosy red sores, which would later burst, leaving behind a golden-crusted scab not unlike a cornflake. It was known as the seven-year itch. The prescribed cure was sulphur, which was used a lot in baths and has the most foul, chemical odour you'll likely ever encounter. The very mention of it sends a shudder down my spine. Though nowadays spas and health farms likely charge a fortune for one to bathe in the stuff.

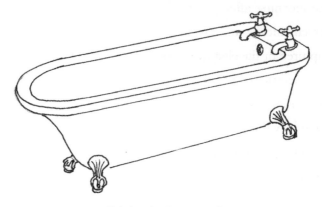

Sulphur bath anyone?

Though effluvious, the smell of sulphur didn't worry us too much in Stockwell as, if the wind was blowing in from Vauxhall, the whiff would be overtaken by that of Sarson's pickle factory and its unforgettable mixture of stale vinegar and onions. I'm not sure which was the lesser of the two evils, but for every sweet-smelling apple pie I encountered I suppose there has to be a foul-smelling pickle somewhere?

I was actually aged eleven-and-three-quarters (the three-quarters being all-important) the day that war was declared, first with the broadcast on the radio by Prime Minister Neville Chamberlain and then with the chimes of Big Ben ringing out across the city. I don't think, as children, we ever appreciated what brutality war inflicts – my friends and I were more interested in picking up bits of shrapnel the morning after an attack. Fortunately, my street wasn't directly hit but we were all affected when the gas mains were ruptured or the electricity lines went down. At one point we had electricity but no gas, so my father turned the electric fire on its side and put a kettle on the bars to boil water! (Don't try this at home, please!)

Perhaps the biggest impact for any child was rationing, particularly the rationing of sweets. Quotas were imposed on everything from petrol, elastic and sugar to bathwater and food. I remember so well the ration books my parents were issued with, and how Mum had to register at specific shops – a butcher, a greengrocer and the like – and had to produce the book to make a purchase, subject to having an allowance, or coupon, left that week. It must seem strange to younger readers to think that we had just eight ounces of butter, one egg, and just over a shilling's worth of meat per week, and just one pound of sweets in any given month,

À bientôt …

❧

You don't get older, you get better.

SHIRLEY BASSEY

❧

often much less. As for fruit, well that wasn't rationed but was extremely hard to come by – and I never saw a banana until 1947.

We were introduced to 'blended' chocolate, which was neither milk nor plain, nor very sweet come to think of it, and consequently it wasn't craved in any large quantities, which perhaps pleased the government.

We were also encouraged to 'Dig for Victory' and grow our own fruit and vegetables and there's no doubt we were healthier for it. There were no processed meats, over-sugared foods and desserts nor were there any leftovers or food waste: everything was planned and everything was used. I'm afraid we didn't dig for victory in our family, though. Our flat did have a garden but it was shared, and as nobody seemed keen on keeping it, it pretty much all fell to weed, I'm ashamed to say.

Nightly blackouts were compulsory in houses, and no light – not even a crack – could be shown to the outside world. One evening my mother was sitting knitting socks on four steel needles in front of the fire and my father was sitting opposite her in his armchair. It was before dark, but they fell asleep, only to be woken by the sound of an air raid warden's whistle and shouts of 'Put that light out! Put that light out!' They both leapt up and my mother dropped her knitting needles to the floor, only for my father to step on two of them, which went directly and quite deeply into his foot – deep enough that he couldn't get a grip on them and couldn't remove them by hand. He limped out to the workshop shed to find a pair of pliers and ... well, I'll leave you to imagine the rest.

The blackout blind.

WHAT IF ...?

Casino Royale (1967)

As far back as June 1964, producer Charles K. Feldman, who owned the rights to Ian Fleming's first James Bond novel, went on record stating he was going to make a movie to rival the Harry Saltzman–Cubby Broccoli productions: 'I want an English actor for the role and the ideal man is Roger Moore.' Apparently, when quizzed by the British press during the production run of *The Saint*, I said: 'I have always fancied myself as Bond and if I'm not too tied up with Simon Templar I shall be delighted to do it.'

Feldman instead chose to make a spoof of the story with David Niven, Peter Sellers and Woody Allen. As for me? Well, I had to bide my time for a decade until I fulfilled my fancy.

I was evacuated for some years but later returned to London towards the end of the war, when I started work. One of the most terrifying daily dangers were the buzz bombs or doodlebugs, from 1944 on. No one was really sure what they were at first, as they weren't dropped from planes, then we began to realize they were in effect self-propelled pilotless aircraft which, when they reached their maximum range, would simply fall out of the sky and deliver their explosive load directly below. They had a strange tearing and rasping sound, a bit like a two-stroke motorcycle engine until, suddenly, the motor cut out and it fell silent – and then you knew it was going to drop nearby and so rushed to take shelter. South London was on their regular flight path and there was a particularly bad incident in July 1944 when a flying bomb fell in the main shopping centre of nearby Lewisham; it penetrated an air raid shelter, causing fifty-one deaths and many casualties.

Soon, they were replaced by the far more frightening V2 rockets, much larger and more destructive, which gave no notice at all of their arrival. At my place of work in D'Arblay Street in the West End of London, we had a rotation list of bomb spotters, which meant we'd have to go up on the roof to watch and listen. When we heard the first faint buzz coming towards us we'd blow whistles to warn everyone in the building to take cover – under a desk usually, though many people used to hide under the stairs, reasoning that whenever you walked down a bombed-out street the stairs were always left standing.

The sight of Big Ben always thrills me.

Big Ben was and still is, of course, one of the defining sights of London and symbols of Britain. It was never silenced during the war, but it did fall dark. Just up the road from the famous clock tower is Buckingham Palace and whenever I'm in that area I think back to before the war, when my parents took me to see the changing of the guard. I could only have been three or four. There, for all to see, were the immaculately turned-out guards with

40

their precision drill and bands playing stirring music – the ceremony is still one of London's most popular attractions, epitomizing the pomp and military ceremony for which Britain is famous. Mum and Dad had just bought me new shoes – sandals – and I remember sidling up to one of the smartly dressed guards in his bright red tunic, big bearskin hat and highly polished shiny black boots. I placed my new sandals alongside his size elevens and, nudging him, exclaimed with great pride, 'Look! New shoes!'

He said something out of the side of his mouth, which I can probably guess was along the lines of 'clear off'. It makes you proud to be British!

Young children have a total innocence about them and often ask what they think are the most logical and innocent questions. I remember one such incident during the war years when I was with my Aunt Nelly on the top of a London bus, going around Trafalgar Square.

'If I started as a seed growing under Mummy's heart, how does the seed get there?' I asked.

Such thoughts of the birds and bees proved highly embarrassing for my dear maiden aunt, who sat silently for the rest of the journey.

My Aunt Nelly always wore a beret with a big long hatpin in it, in case of any unwanted attention. Sure enough, one night at the picture house in the Elephant and Castle, a fellow started moving his leg in towards hers and, what's more, then placed his hand on her leg, without so much as a 'Hello, how are you?' She kept calm, casually reached up to her hat, removed the pin and, with all the force she could muster, stabbed it deep into his thigh. He screamed and ran out, with the needle still embedded, never to be seen again. I dare say he never got to see the film again, either.

Sadly, cinemas did attract an element of the 'wrong sort' – or perverts, if you prefer. On another outing, my mother was at the Brixton Empress with my father, and a man on the other side of my mother started moving his hand along the top of her leg. She leant towards my father and said, 'George, this man is touching me.'

The man realized she was talking to her husband and quickly jumped up to leave, but my father was faster. He jumped over a row of seats and cornered him. Grabbing the chap around the throat he said, 'You've picked the wrong woman here, you silly bugger!' and, if it hadn't been for the usherettes pulling him off, my father may well have throttled him.

Aunt Nelly later married a chap called Peter Collis who, as a child, while hanging onto the back of a moving cart, fell off and broke his thighbone. After doctors had reset the bone, he sadly developed osteomyelitis, a very nasty infection, and eventually Peter had to have the leg amputated. They replaced it with a metal limb and although he could walk with it fine, he couldn't control it when sitting down. One day on the bus a woman suddenly screamed, 'You dirty beast!' His false leg had leaned sideways and was touching her leg. He rapped on it with his knuckles, showing her it was hollow, and she was just as embarrassed as he was. So that goes to show that while some may deserve punishment, not all leg-touchers are up to no good.

Ah, the wicked weed. A filthy habit – but *so* cool.

Before the end of the war I, sadly (well, I wasn't sad at the time!), started smoking. It was seen as the thing to do back then, and in every film you would generally see the leading man or lady with a cigarette, looking all sexy and alluring. Regular brands were in high demand and consequently hard to get hold of, and I'd often have to make do with a 'mixed' packet containing two Turkish, two Woodbine, two camel dung (well, it tasted like it); or, if I was lucky, a pack of Joystick, which were eight inches long and the tobacconist cut them in half. When I had a bit of extra dosh, I graduated to Passing Cloud and liked people to notice them by lighting up and wafting them around very publicly on the top deck of the bus. Ah! The bad old days, when it was acceptable to inhale the filthy weed. I suppose after many years of rationing and shortages, we all craved a bit of luxury and sadly found it in a fag packet. Now, of course, we know too well how damaging they are to our bodies and to our health, and I actually find the smell quite repulsive these days – there's nothing worse than a smoker talking up close to you, the smell on their breath, their clothes … awful!

Another war that has played a big part in my life has been the Cold War. Having been embroiled, on screen at least, with the Cold War over many years as Jimmy Bond, the world suddenly changed for the better when the Berlin Wall fell in 1989. Following World War II, there was very much a 'them and us' feeling between the Western world and the Eastern Bloc of the Soviet Union and its states, and I think it probably reached its scariest height in the late 1950s and early 1960s.

Politics and filmmaking – a toxic mix in 1950s.

I remember in 1957, politics raised its head at Warner Bros when a film crew came over from Russia to coincide with the premiere of *The Cranes Are Flying* – an important World War II film from the Soviet point of view. The right-wing studio executives weren't best pleased that we were to be 'overrun by communists' and, in the wake of McCarthyism, none of the Warner Bros contract players would have their pictures taken with the Soviets for fear of having their political leanings questioned or, worse still, being blacklisted for work. I thought it was crazy – we were all filmmakers, after all – and so insisted that Dorothy Provine, who was filming *The Alaskans* with me, and I would come to lunch with our visitors. We were the only two westerners in the commissary that day.

The JFK–Richard Nixon presidential election of 1960 also sticks in my mind. It was Nixon's first election run and we contract players were 'requested' by the Warner Bros management to vote for him as our best bet against communism spreading – not that I had a vote as a foreigner! This was a remarkable election for many reasons but I was fascinated by the televised debate between the two, the first debate of its kind, which pitched the handsome Kennedy up against the much more experienced vice-president Nixon. However, on the night Nixon was nervous and sweaty, especially in front of the TV cameras. It just shows you the power of television, as apparently if you listened on the radio you thought Nixon had won, but if you watched it on TV, Kennedy was the obvious choice – take heed politicians! Nixon learned his lesson: after a bit of coaching, when he successfully stood for office again in 1969, he gently wiped his lips with a handkerchief every now and again.

So, back in 1961, Kennedy was sworn in as President and the following year, in October 1962, the Cuban Missile Crisis presented the West with a thirteen-day scare. I was in Europe making the first series of *The Saint* by then, but remember so well the TV and media reports of how Russia had installed

Jimmy Bond on the Berlin Wall in 1983.
(© 1962-2017 Danjaq LLC and United Artists Corp.)

missiles in communist Cuba, just ninety miles off the coast of Florida, which could have been operational within two weeks and risked sparking World War III. Mercifully, it was avoided.

The Cold War period and communism was certainly a worry, as there was always a threat of nuclear war hanging over us all, and some questioned if it would ever thaw so that we might live in relative harmony. We lived in hope, but it didn't seem terribly likely.

Having filmed in Berlin, alongside the dividing wall, in 1983, I had my own first-hand glimpse at just how the Iron

Curtain had split a great city. A mere six years later the wall fell, the death knell of the Cold War and communism was sounded and the free movement of people across Germany was swiftly followed by reunification.

Right now, the forty-year membership the UK has enjoyed within the EU (EEC and Common Market, as was) is coming to an end. The people spoke, and the majority called for an exit. It has saddened me because I always thought it was a good move, bringing Europe closer together. Although I am proudly British, I've always thought of myself as a European too – after all, I've lived in France and Monaco since the late 1970s – and fervently believe that by coming together as member states of the EU we avoided another world war. Living and trading together in harmony has seen borders open and prices fall.

On an everyday level, being part of the EU has seen the establishment of guaranteed rights for workers; it gave new fathers the right to paid paternity leave; low-cost flights were suddenly possible and family holidays affordable; it's seen mobile phone operators drop relay charges so you can use your phones for calls and data roaming just as you would at home ... and while yes, I agree, the EU hasn't got everything right, I do believe more good than bad has come out of the UK being a member state.

❧

*The older I get, the more open-minded I get,
the less judgmental I get.*

GWYNETH PALTROW

❧

Though Britain never joined the euro, I do remember the last major upheaval in our currency when we turned decimal in 1971, though for those aged under fifty it will be hard to imagine accounting in pounds, shillings and pence! The old system I grew up with had twelve pennies in a shilling and twenty shillings in a pound. It was complex arithmetic we all wrestled with at times, but it was a system people were reluctant to see disappear. While there was much puzzlement getting used to the new pounds and pence, and claims of shops rounding *up* prices rather than taking them *down* to the nearest halfpenny, we all seemed to cope. However, I still can't get used to metric weights and measures. When I'm asked my height in metres, I'm afraid really don't know. I think it's 1.83m. Weight: 12.5 stone – what am I in kilos? I'm not too sure, something like 80?

Answers on a postcard, please!

All I can say is, I'm glad I wasn't at the front!

THE JOY
OF TRAVELLING

Once upon a time, travelling was a real joy and something to look forward to. People used to hop into their cars for an evening or afternoon drive out, without fear of cameras clocking them making a wrong turn or entering a yellow box by an inch too much, both resulting in a fine arriving in the post. Certainly there is little joy nowadays in driving a car around London – or any big city – what with congestion charges, bus lanes and prohibited manoeuvres, though my dear departed friend Michael Winner used to say, 'Bus lanes are marvellous, there's hardly any traffic using them and it only costs me sixty pounds!'

I remember friends who used to take an evening drive out to London Airport (now Heathrow) for dinner and to enjoy the surroundings. Can you imagine doing that now? For one thing the parking charges would be more than the cost of a meal.

I also remember a wonderful day out, in the early 1970s, when I was invited to drive down towards Swindon with my children Geoffrey and Deborah to visit a brand new Concorde plane. It hadn't yet come into service, but they were taking some test flights and invited people to join them on short trips. Sadly, when we got there the flight was cancelled for weather reasons, but we were shown all around the plane and were totally awe-inspired.

My first-ever flight was to New York in 1952. They were the days of flying in style aboard BOAC (the British Overseas Airways Corporation), where the stewards wore white gloves and there were proper sleeper seats. Oh, and there was a bar downstairs! You couldn't fly directly, and had to stop off in Greenland or Iceland to refuel. I guess you were talking about twelve hours on board in all.

I remember being on the first non-stop flight from New York to Los Angeles in 1953, and as we approached the Rockies the pilot said, 'We've lost an engine! I could go on but would rather not!' So we landed in Denver. The flight behind us – the second non-stop flight – was then made to land in Denver too, and the passengers were asked to get off to allow us to continue. They really resented that!

Airports are not my favourite places now, I'm afraid. Back in the 'golden age of travel', it felt really luxurious and passengers were welcomed aboard as customers. Ah, to hark back to those heady days when Concorde was in the skies. Now, I really don't look forward to flying on commercial airlines at all. There's no joy in queuing up to check in, before joining another queue for the security lane then on to another queue to board the plane.

I know security is for our own benefit but more often than not you're barked at by staff in whatever language they speak in said country, and the delivery is always curt: 'Take your coat off, shoes off, belt off, empty your pockets ...'

Having experienced this just recently, and seeing the plastic trays with my worldly belongings moving off towards the scanner as I was left holding up my trousers with one hand, I explained I have a pacemaker and could not go through the metal detector.

'Where's your card?' the person asked curtly, referring to the proof of my pacemaker.

'In my wallet – over there,' I pointed to the plastic tray disappearing into the machine.

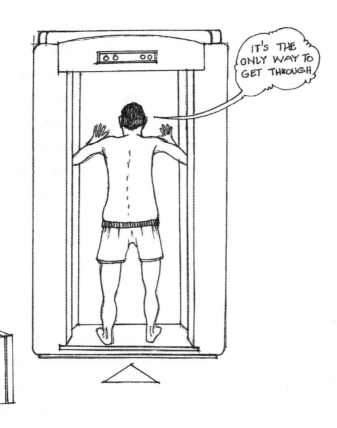

A 'tut' and a shake of the head was then followed by another bark of, 'Come this way,' as the man led me to the full body scanner.

'Put your hands up here, above your shoulders,' he said.

'I can't,' I replied, gripping my waistband tightly. 'My trousers will fall down!' Cue the onlookers getting their camera phones at the ready.

*One of the good things about getting older
is you find you're more interesting than
most of the people you meet.*

LEE MARVIN

So they escorted me to another area where they had a
hand-held metal detector, which they proceeded to rub all
over me, before giving me a pat down and agreeing that I
posed no threat.

'OK,' he said, as he gestured me on.

Of course, you have to tuck all your liquids, ointments,
medication and other toiletries into a small, clear plastic bag;
in goes the toothpaste, eye drops, my blood pressure pills,
laxatives, Imodium (in case the laxatives prove too effective),
aspirin, paracetamol, haemorrhoid cream, that stuff for dry
lips and so on. But oh, wait! There's one thing over 100ml!
And so at the *other* side of the scanner they wanted me to
empty out all my belongings in front of everyone so they
could poke through them. How embarrassing! I mean, I
don't want people to think I have dry lips.

Panic over – the culprit was a larger-than-average tube of toothpaste. That had to be dispensed with forthwith.

As I say, I know security is for our own safety but has courtesy and politeness gone out the window?

At big airports, with mile-long corridors and concourses, I usually ask if I can have a little golf buggy. My old knees aren't as good as they once were and it makes life so much easier. Sometimes it's not possible and they offer a wheelchair. I'm not terribly keen on taking one as invariably a sea of camera phones appears on my route, all snapping away. I can see the *Daily Mail* headlines now: '007 TRADES IN LOTUS ESPRIT FOR WHEELCHAIR'.

However, on a recent trip out of Nice I had a slightly swollen ankle, and my wife, Kristina, was adamant I shouldn't aggravate it by walking further than I had to, and so I accepted a wheelchair ride. I think the operative had been in training for the Monaco Grand Prix, as she pushed me so fast that Kristina couldn't keep up and I found myself waving furiously and calling a warning to the people ahead, 'Mind out of the way!'

We had allocated seats so thought we'd board after the mad rush, but my pusher had other ideas and parted the crowds at the check-in desk, 'Pardon! Pardon!'

It brought a whole new meaning to speedy boarding.

On another recent flight, this time to Belfast, we booked the front two row A seats, as they offered a bit more leg room for my large frame in the tiny prop-jet plane. My two associates, Gareth and Mike, were in row B behind us. As we climbed up the few steps to board there was a bit of muttering and the cabin steward asked Kristina and me to swap with Mike and Gareth and sit in row B.

'No, we're in row B,' said Gareth, politely. 'We purposely booked row A seats for them.'

The steward was nonplussed and insisted we swap. When pushed as to why, she replied, 'Well, they are rather elderly. Row A is an exit row, and I'm concerned they'd hinder other passengers in an emergency.'

Such charm!

So, we two 'elderly folk' – aware of a whole plane-full of faces staring at us – took row B.

After landing, as we gathered our bits and pieces from the overhead locker, Kristina quietly leaned in to the steward and said, 'I used to do your job on SAS airlines. For many years. If you want someone to be a help during an emergency an ex-cabin steward would be much better in row A surely?'

Such a sweet statement, delivered in a cool, calm yet assured manner. It caused the steward to go bright red and apologize profusely. Just because we are of an age doesn't mean we're totally decrepit.

Of course, we landed at the furthest end of the airport and were all forced to filter through various doors, queues and long, long corridors to the exit. Sorry, let me stop here just one minute and ask, why does that always happen? Why, whatever plane one boards, is it without exception at the gate furthest away from the airport terminal, and always lands at the gate furthest from the terminal you are visiting? Is it just me? I often wonder that.

I digress. Once we reached the exit, we had to walk back along the same route, though on the other side of the wall, to meet our driver, who turned out to be parked directly opposite the plane, albeit with a big barbed-wire fence between it and him. Had we scaled it, it would have saved half an hour of walking.

Still, it's better than having to board a bus at the plane door and being driven around the airport aimlessly for twenty minutes looking for a way out, as was our next experience in Manchester, but that's a book on its own.

Have you tried paying for parking in any big city lately? Gone are the days when you popped coins into parking meters, now you have to pay by text or app. Of course, what they don't tell you is that first you have to set up an account with your payment card, which in itself takes twenty minutes, entering all the details before you're prompted for the car registration number. Like many others, I don't have my registration number committed to memory, so I had to step out into the road to read it and then wait for a confirmation that we were legally parked – by which time our lunch meeting was looking like more of an afternoon tea gathering.

What on earth happens if you don't have a mobile phone with you or the network is down? Do they make other provisions? No!

One of the great joys of travelling as an older person is that in some places you get a bus pass. In London they call it a Freedom Pass, though I still haven't come to terms with what 'touching in' is all about as you get on board. Once upon a time you simply paid the conductor. Once upon a time you actually *looked* at the conductor and smiled – sometimes even engaging in short conversational pleasantries. Nowadays you simply flash your credentials at them. Though flashing is not permitted, of course.

I've always enjoyed travelling by train, which seems one of the more civilized ways of moving from A to B, and I must admit it also enables Kristina and I to play cards

– sometimes she even lets me win. I've travelled by train in the UK quite extensively of late, and must admit that the special services division of the network was brilliant in helping this old boy with getting on/off the trains and through the stations. Better still, it's a service they provide for free if booked in advance.

I enjoyed a couple of train trips as Jimmy Bond – first in *Live and Let Die* and then in *The Spy Who Loved Me* – though I had to dispatch two villains out of the windows, which made them a little draughty. Later on I was enticed into working on *Bullseye!* with Michael Caine with the promise of

I love the old London Routemaster buses – especially now I have my Freedom Pass.

filming on board the *Orient Express* travelling down to Venice, but budget cuts saw us on the Pullman travelling through Scotland instead!

On one recent book tour we took the ICE train in Germany from Berlin to Hamburg and then to Cologne and it was joyous. We had delicious meals, served at our seats, and I've always marvelled at just how good the food is on board a train with the chef operating in a tiny, narrow kitchen, travelling at over 200mph. We arrived in Cologne feeling happy and relaxed, only to find that we had obviously been spotted boarding in Hamburg, as by the time we reached the train's final destination an entire posse of autograph hunters was awaiting our arrival on the platform – with arms full of multiple photos, DVDs and books that required no dedications, only signatures. 'eBay here we come!' I thought.

It's funny but whenever I board a train I still fear using the WC while stationary, as we were always told as youngsters that it wasn't allowed. Without wishing to sound indelicate, it was because the WC emptied onto the track – and no one wants to put up with a smelly station. Is that still the case? I must remember to ask someone who might know … Sorry, I don't know why my thoughts have dragged me back to the smallest room once more.

❧

I intend to live forever, or die trying.

GROUCHO MARX

❧

Having lived in London throughout my formative years I was very well acquainted with the Underground or Tube system. What a brilliant engineering achievement underneath the capital's streets and the River Thames. Those pioneering 1920s genius engineers made so much possible. Modern engineers can also take a bow. One of the most impressive pieces of British engineering in my lifetime is the Channel Tunnel, which is over thirty-one miles long. It's been recognized as one of the Seven Wonders of the Modern World by the American Society of Civil Engineers (alongside the Empire State Building, the Itaipu Dam in South America, the CN Tower in Toronto, the Panama Canal, the North Sea protection works – dykes – in the Netherlands, and the Golden Gate Bridge in San Francisco).

There had been talk, going back over a hundred years, of a Channel Tunnel that might one day allow trains to travel beneath the sea between Britain and France. In

1935, Gaumont Studios produced a film called *The Tunnel*, a futuristic science fiction story concerning the creation of a transatlantic tunnel in which it mentioned in passing that a Channel Tunnel had already been completed. But in reality we had to wait until 1988 for construction to start.

It is a genuine marvel that it takes just a few hours from the heart of London to the centre of Paris, but the thing that always strikes me is that I can never find a porter or a luggage trolley at the Gare du Nord – you arrive with your bags and have to drag them up and down the platform to and from the taxi ranks. Such engineering, such technology – yet not a porter in sight!

Man's best friend seems to have seen something more interesting.

WHAT MIGHT HAVE BEEN

I'm often asked if I had my life over again, is there anything I'd do differently? As I don't own a crystal ball or have the ability to see what's around the corner, I don't think I could have really made different choices at the time, as I believed I'd already made the best judgements. I also think it would be terribly ungrateful if I were to say yes and start listing things, as I've had such a wonderful and fun life. Each moment – whether it be good or bad, happy or sad – has had a bearing and influence on making me who I am today. Yes, I'd certainly happily avoid instances of kidney stones, but do I regret the career decisions I made? On the whole, no. However, decisions are not always entirely your own choice. Sometimes things happen, circumstances arise and coincidences take you off on a predetermined path, whether you're aware of it at the time or not.

For example, and bear with me here, I'm going back a bit. Once, while visiting that same cinema where Aunt Nelly plunged her hatpin deep into the man's leg, I fainted. No, it was nothing to do with a girl doing similar to me, thank you very much, but it was while I was in a twelve-abreast queue outside to see *The Drum* starring Sabu, in 1938. I was only a lad, and the fainting was probably simply caused by being momentarily starved of oxygen in the crowd – but it turned out to be a good move on my part because I got in for free.

The Drum was a terrific film, produced by the great Sir Alexander Korda, who inadvertently played a major part in my career by building Denham Studios in Buckinghamshire. That was where I made my fateful first appearance on film, as a spear-carrying extra in *Caesar and Cleopatra* (1945), and launched my career as an actor. Perhaps more significantly, he was responsible for setting Lewis Gilbert on his path as a director – and as director of two of my Bond films in the 1970s I have so much to be grateful for with regard to Lewis.

WHAT IF ...?

Clubbing

Although not a film, I thought I'd also mention a story that ran in the *Evening News* in 1964.

'Mr Roger Moore the actor, star of *The Saint* TV series, tells me he has given up the idea he had of opening a club in Majorca. "I decided that with all my TV commitments, Majorca would really be too far away to allow me to keep my eye on things", he told me from the terrace of his holiday hotel, the Flamboya, at Magaluf. Instead, Mr Moore, in partnership with Mr Davy Kaye the comedian, is to open a club in London. "We shall provide good entertainment and good food in addition to gambling facilities," Mr Moore grinned. "Opening a club like this will be a big gamble, but Davy and I are inveterate gamblers and aim to win!"'

What crap! Mind you, serves that reporter right for disturbing me on my holiday. Oh well, he wanted a story and I gave him one. Who knows, I might have become Johnny Gold?!

The Spy Who Loved Me (1977) was the very best Bond film I made, and Lewis's second with me, *Moonraker* (1979), was the most commercially successful 007 outing for decades, earning me a handy few bob along the way.

How did it come about? Well, the story goes that Lewis had formerly been a child actor and appeared in *The Divorce of Lady X* (1938), which was produced by Sir Alex. One day on set, the great filmmaker said to Lewis, 'Young man you're going through a transition where you're going to be too old to play children, and too young to play adult parts. So you have to think about your future. What do you want to do?'

Lewis thought for a moment and said he'd like to be an assistant director.

'Report to Denham Studios on Monday,' said Korda, and that was the beginning for Lewis, who soon, in fact, progressed to directing documentary shorts and then features. Roll on a decade or more and one of the last films Korda had some sort of involvement in was *The Admirable Crichton* (1957), which Lewis directed. During preparation, Korda was chatting with Lewis and asked how he started out.

'Well, sir, I was a child actor and you asked me what I wanted to do …'

'My God!' cried Korda. 'You were that little boy?'

'Yes, and thank you!' said Lewis.

Two days later, Lewis had an appointment with Korda and called the office to confirm, but the secretary said the meeting had been cancelled – Sir Alex had died the night before. Lewis said he was so grateful to have been able to say thank you to the man who launched his career.

*Old age is always fifteen
years older than I am.*

OLIVER WENDELL HOLMES

Incidentally, during World War II my old mate David Niven had a rolling contract with Korda, who even back then owned the film rights to *The Admirable Crichton* (it's a J. M. Barrie stage play), and the producer was keen that Niven play the lead. In order to raise the finance, Korda sent a telegram to Sam Goldwyn at MGM: SUGGEST YOU DO, FOR WAR EFFORT, ADMIRAL CRICHTON.

He thought it was a story set in the navy and hadn't even read it!

Korda's knighthood wasn't for services to the film industry, but actually for his work in British intelligence –

what better cover is there than a film producer, who has to travel to many different countries to set up pictures? No one suspected he was a spy.

I can't but help thinking, what if Korda hadn't started making films, and what if he hadn't cast a young Lewis Gilbert and offered him that advice? Where might I be now?

When I got my first job from school, as a lowly animator, I believed it to be the best day of my life: the day I was fired probably ranked as the worst. But from that bit of bad luck I was able to join some mates doing crowd work at Denham Studios, which ultimately led to a seven-year contract with MGM in Hollywood. When it was cut short after just a few years I thought I'd never work again – it was the worst possible news. Yet I'd challenge anyone not to believe things happen for a reason, as that piece of bad luck led me to a contract with Columbia to make *Ivanhoe* on television, which in turn led to a contract with Warner Bros. And following that came a couple of awful films in Italy, where I met the mother of my children. Had Warner's not fired me I'd never have gone to Rome, and likely wouldn't have Deborah, Geoffrey and Christian now.

Had those films in Italy been any good, I may have made

more of them. But as it happens I didn't and that meant I was free to play Simon Templar in *The Saint*.

My greatest and proudest acting role, of course, came a little later with James Bond. Thirty-odd years after leaving the series I'm still delighted to be part of it all, and sitting here now wondering 'what if?', I think of Ian Fleming sitting

Pinewood Studios was 'home' to me for longer than I care to remember.

down at his Jamaican retreat, putting a piece of paper into his golden typewriter, and starting work on the first Bond novel, *Casino Royale*. Everything thereafter, totally unknown to me at the time, set the ball rolling towards my incarnation of the role across seven films:

- What if Harry Saltzman hadn't optioned the books?
- What if Albert R. Broccoli hadn't met Harry Saltzman and ran with the option, raising finance at United Artists?
- What if Sean Connery hadn't made five, and then walked away?
- What if George Lazenby had signed a seven-year contract and hadn't quit after just one film?
- After Sean returned, what if he hadn't refused to make any more Bonds after the one-off (as he saw it) *Diamonds Are Forever* (1971)?

At any step of the way, things could have turned out so very differently – though what would be the odds of a policeman's son from south London playing the world's most famous spy in a series of multi-million-dollar movies? I wish I'd had a pound on it!

"My family is my life."

FAMILY

One of the greater blessings of reaching an advanced age is in being able to see your children and grandchildren grow up and prosper. Oh! And since my last book, I have another granddaughter too – Maria Luisa – who was born at the end of November 2015 to Lara and Christian.

More than anything else, saying my two eldest children are in their fifties makes me feel old. I'm not sure Deborah and Geoffrey appreciate me referring to them as middle-aged in conversation, particularly as it only seems like yesterday they were running around the school playground, but being children of the 1960s, I'm afraid they are now pushing on a bit – though far be it from me to rub it in.

I've always thought of myself as fairly upstanding, honest and loyal. They are traits I instilled in my children and in my grandchildren too. However, there are times when little white lies, to save hurting feelings, are permissible. There are also times when for fear of saying something unkind or unfortunate, you should keep your mouth shut. I learned this from my Aunt Amy. She was just a couple of years older than my mother, and when I was seven or eight – I suppose she was in her late thirties – I asked her why she didn't shave.

I got a whack round the back of my neck. 'Yeah, but, she *has* got a moustache so why not shave it?' I got another whack.

Lesson learned.

Amy owned a parrot, which despite being called Polly, was presumed to be male. Amy would always say 'he' said this and 'he' did that. Then one day 'he' laid an egg – which was probably just as much of a shock to the bird as it was to Amy.

My extended family is a little more complicated and widespread than my immediate. My maternal grandfather, the father of Nellie, Jack, Amy and my mother Lily, was widowed relatively young and eventually remarried – to his first wife's half-sister, meaning his former sister-in-law

72

became his wife. They had three children together, two boys and a girl – Peter, Bob and Nancy. Those children felt like my cousins as I was almost the same age as them, but they were technically my aunt and uncle and always insisted I call them that!

The closeness of the family sadly evaporated due to the war, and we all went in different directions. Tragically, in 1944 Jack was killed in Monte Cassino. We all kept in touch at Christmas time, but after my mother and father died we never really met up, apart from at funerals, and sadly my aunts and uncles have now all gone. No more whacks around the head for me.

I was always close to Kristina's daughter, Christina (who we called Flossie, to avoid confusion), and had known her since she was a teenager. After Kristina and I married, Flossie often came to stay, or she would meet up with us on our travels around the world. I use the past tense because she died in 2016, leaving a huge hole in our lives.

In November 2015, Flossie accompanied Kristina and I on one of our trips – to Vienna. My darling wife was being recognized at the annual Woman of the Year Awards, in the 'Strong Woman' category. Behind every seemingly strong man is a stronger woman and I've always said that Kristina makes a better UNICEF ambassador than me: she always asks to meet the disabled children, who are invariably hidden away, and chats with them, spends time with them and tries to show that there is no stigma attached to children who are not perceived as being 'normal' due to physical or mental health issues. Kristina is my tower of strength.

Kristina at the Woman of the Year Awards in 2015.

Normally my shy and modest wife would have shunned such an award, seeing it as very nice, but not for her. However, on this occasion I persuaded her to think about it because I knew it was hugely deserved recognition for everything she does so quietly and privately. She never takes part in interviews, always politely turns down requests to speak and, though happy to be at my side, always pushes the spotlight for such tasks onto me.

To my delight, on this occasion Kristina agreed to receive the award, on condition that I'd be there with her. I was actually asked to read the citation, detailing why she

was being bestowed the honour, before bringing her onto the huge stage at the beautiful Rathaus building in Vienna, where a thousand or more people had arrived to the gala dinner. Flossie was very keen to be with us and to see her mother publicly honoured, so flew out for a couple of days. On arrival, Flossie told me she was keen to speak about her mother on stage that night. I explained that wasn't possible as everything was tightly programmed and arranged, and that adding another speech wasn't really appropriate – Flossie loved to make speeches! She was quite insistent, as was I, and while we didn't fall out, there was a bit of an atmosphere in the car heading over to the City Hall. Oh, how I regret it now.

Flossie was seated adjacent to us for the dinner, but we noticed she left soon after her mother had received her award. I thought perhaps she was still a little upset with me, but back at the hotel she explained she'd felt a little tired and had, after all, been travelling pretty much all day from her home near Cheltenham, via London, to be with us.

The next day I commented her complexion looked a little pale. No, not pale, yellow. She thought it was highly hilarious and started posting photos on her Facebook page saying, 'Ooh, look at me! I'm all yellow!'

I suggested she should see a doctor, but she dismissed it, saying she was too busy and was sure it would be fine in a day or two. Kristina and I nagged her to see a doctor on her return to London, and after another day or two had passed with no improvement she relented. Her doctor in turn referred her to another doctor and it was then that the devastating news was revealed: an aggressive, terminal cancer.

I can't begin to tell you the pain, anguish and tears we all shared. Poor Flossie's mother was inconsolable with the shock of hearing her daughter had an illness that could, at best, be treated to give her a few more precious months, maybe a year, possibly two.

In fact, she lived just over six months.

In those final weeks and months we were pretty much together all the time, either at our chalet in Switzerland or with her in Cheltenham at her beautiful house 'Windrush', where she stabled her horses and lived with her four beloved dogs. We knew every day, every hour and every minute were precious and were determined we would make the most of what time she had left.

Through round after round of treatment, travelling back and forth to London, Flossie remained bullish, brave and fiercely determined. She was particularly buoyed by one of her eventing horses, 'Wesko', being selected for the 2016 Olympics, though a few months later, an injury to its leg resulted in it having to be withdrawn. That was a big sadness.

Flossie was terribly brave and refused to give in – she was nothing if not headstrong. She had achieved so very many things in her forty-odd years, more than most people might in eighty years, and if ever there was a consolation it was in knowing she had lived life to the full and enjoyed every minute.

The bastard cancer finally took her from us in July 2016. I never imagined anyone could cry so much as Kristina did.

And in the end, it's not the years in your life that count. It's the life in your years.

ABRAHAM LINCOLN

In the final weeks, when she started growing weaker, Flossie wanted to make sure all her affairs were in order and taken care of. Her horses and dogs were the first priority, and our dear Danish friends Kate and Carsten immediately volunteered to adopt the dogs and oversee the care and sale of the horses. They took such a weight off Flossie's shoulders. Our good friend Janus Friis had been there for Flossie going back many years, and continues to be now for us in securing her legacy by establishing an equestrian centre in her name.

With Flossie and Kristina in Vienna.

No parent should have to bury a child. It's the cruellest, most awful thing you can ever imagine. Kristina was unable to speak at the funeral – it was all she could do to be there in the face of horrific grief – but she asked that I share some personal memories of Flossie and I think these two, which I read at her funeral, sum her up:

When Flossie was about sixteen she was travelling to Berlin with her school when they were stopped at the border crossing by the East German police. There was a bit of a kerfuffle. Flossie's passport photo had been tampered with and changed, and not very professionally either. The train was held up for seven or eight hours waiting for the Stasi to arrive and investigate. Flossie freely admitted she'd changed the photograph, which obviously set alarm bells ringing. On being asked why, she replied matter-of-factly, 'Because I didn't like the old photo!'

The second incident occurred in the hospital, during her final week. A group of doctors came into her room to talk things through and update us, and as they started to shuffle out, Flossie asked one of them to stay behind. She beckoned him closer, and whispered quietly, 'Your breath smells.' The next day, he arrived sucking on a mint.

That was Flossie. She was truly unique.

I loved gadgets from an early age – but look at the size of that camera.

THE OLD GREY MATTER AND TECHNOLOGY

I can quote Shakespearean sonnets that I learned at RADA in 1940-something. I can remember lines from plays I performed in repertory theatre, and whole chunks of dialogue from films I haven't seen since their premiere. I can tell you the best route from London's Wardour Street to Battersea, road name by road name ... So why is it I sometimes stand in the kitchen wondering what I went in there for?

I liken the brain to a Rolodex filing system. The older

you get, the more information the Rolodex has to store and therefore the laws of physics state it takes a little longer to find exactly what you're looking for when you go rummaging. Sounds convincing, to me at least.

As you get older three things happen. The first is your memory goes, and I can't remember the other two.

SIR NORMAN WISDOM

I've always loved gadgets. I was in seventh heaven trying out all the various watches, cameras, cars and gizmos as Jimmy Bond. Consequently, I'm quite savvy when it comes to the internet and my Mac, iPhone and iPad. Google is a doddle, email is time-saving, Facetime and Skype are wonderful for saving on the phone bill, but for some unknown reason my various machines and tablets occasionally seem to forget the all-important login password, so I dutifully tap it in again only for an 'error' message to appear. There are only so many 'errors' you're allowed before the whole thing goes slightly apocalyptic and threatens you with a fate worse than death – that of not being able to use your phone.

I usually end up resetting the password and, because I like to have the same password for each online account and service (yes, I know I shouldn't but ...), I go through the tiresome process of updating my Skype, my email, my Amazon, my iTunes, my British Airways ... and all my other passwords to the new one. Later in the week I can guarantee one of the devices will ask me to enter the new password again, before saying it's not recognized – and so the whole routine starts all over. I don't know if I'm unique in managing to upset my devices and make them react in such a manner?

In Switzerland I have a very helpful 'techie' guy who will pop round if I call him, though he only speaks French and my grasp of the language isn't too bad until you get down to technicalities. God knows, it's hard enough in English. So, although he usually resolves the problem, I can't always remember how he did it or what caused it in the first place.

Occasionally, I decide to call one of the so-called technology 'helplines'. Living between Switzerland and Monaco has its advantages, but one of the downsides – as hinted above – is that the people on the other end of the line usually speak German, Italian or French. I pick my way through the issue in my very best pidgin, only for them to answer at a hundred miles an hour and totally flummox me.

WHAT IF ...?

Camelot

In early 1965 I was offered the lead in the West End production of *Camelot* at Drury Lane. It had opened in the August of the previous year, with Laurence Harvey playing Arthur; he was leaving to move on to other projects.

Unfortunately it was mid-production in the latest series of *The Saint* and the dates just didn't work for my schedule, so I had to turn it down. Paul Daneman, who had toured in the part in Australia, replaced Laurence Harvey and, of course, Richard Harris later assumed the lead and went on to star in the film version. Richard toured for six years with the show, reportedly giving him great wealth. In fact, in 1990 he said: 'I couldn't spend my money in five lifetimes.'

That'll upset my bank manager. And to think, I might have gone on to become Dumbledore in the Harry Potter films!

So I usually give up and start the password reset process all over again. Then it all works fine ... until a message appears that tells me I've been disconnected from the wi-fi network.

'What's the wi-fi password?' I'm asked.

How the hell do I know? Some idiot keeps changing it!

Thinking I'll be clever, once I'm back in, I email myself all the new passwords. There they are, in black and white for future reference, though then there is the issue of not being able to get into my email to check on the password when I'm locked out again.

I have a little carry-on suitcase that I always take with me on my travels, and it contains a range of chargers, adaptors, batteries, leads and SIM cards. I have my French iPhone, my Swiss iPhone and a couple of old spare phones for use in other countries – but which SIM card goes in which? I seem to have about four UK pay-as-you-go SIM cards and it's potluck as to which one works once I arrive in London. I've been known to tell everyone I'll be on my Giffgaff number only to discover I'm on my Three number – no wonder my agent never calls me.

Have you tried topping up a pay-as-you-go SIM card? In truth, having endured a flight, a strip-search at the airport and then a drive into London, where all I want to do is unpack and put my feet up for half an hour, I don't relish the idea of trekking out to find a newsagent to buy a voucher, nor similarly to find an ATM, so I usually try to top up online, from the comfort of my armchair. Hah! Questions come up, such as 'What is your login password?'

'Take your pick, mate!'

I become so frustrated that I end up calling them. Even over the phone they ask me questions, such as 'What is your security password?' Look, I can't even get the right SIM card, let alone remember what word I used in 2008 to set up the damn thing. All I want to do is spend some money to top up the wretched card, but they won't let me. I can only imagine how my attempting to load £25 without full security clearance could be misconstrued as money laundering to these companies, but I assure them that I really do have better things to do.

Oh, and have you tried getting a SIM card out of an iPhone? You need a little needle-like probe that slips into a hole, which in turn releases the little tray in which the card sits – but who carries that around with them? So many times have I asked waiters, bar staff, hotel front desks and even taxi drivers if they have a paperclip I can use, only to be a little over-enthusiastic and press it in so hard that the ruddy card tray flies off into a far corner somewhere.

I must try to remain calm.

My first mobile phone was the size of a large house brick – not particularly mobile, I know – and you'd often see people walking down the road like the Hunchback of Notre Dame holding onto these huge weights that were pulling them down. I've probably still got mine upstairs in the house, as I rarely throw anything away. It took hours to charge and the battery didn't last very long and quite honestly the signal would often cut out too, not to mention how horrendously expensive it was to make a call. Though for someone like me who thought direct dial telephone numbers were state of the art, it was a huge novelty and something to show off to friends.

I don't believe one grows older. I think that what happens early on in life is that at a certain age one stands still and stagnates.

T. S. ELIOT

In the pre-mobile phone days, it was fairly difficult to get quick messages to far-flung places of the world, and we relied on telegrams and telex. I remember Billy Wilder saying he was in Paris filming *One, Two, Three* (1961) and

87

Audrey Hepburn sent him a telex asking him to bring back a bidet. His reply: 'CAN'T FIND BIDET. STOP. SUGGEST YOU STAND ON HEAD IN SHOWER.'

But then in the late 1960s came the fax machine. It was probably the 1980s before they became more affordable, and I remember buying one for communications with my agent, lawyer, producers. Film contracts would come whirring through for review, pages of scripts could be changed and transmitted in seconds, and office life suddenly became a lot easier, though we didn't quite realize that the thermal paper on which faxes were printed would fade over the course of a few months – I have a folder full of blank paper contracts! As they say, 'not worth the paper they're written on'.

I had a bit of fun communicating with my son Christian when he was based in LA. With the time difference it wasn't always easy to talk on the phone, so I'd send him notes and updates on family life – though I'd often Tipp-Ex out every few words, so all he received were four words and five blanks per line. Oh, what fun!

I bought a home movie camera and VCR when they first came onto the market. To have a video camera you could hold in your hand was revolutionary and being a would-be director, I filmed hours of footage with the family, on trips, at home – hundreds of tapes. In fact I had it with me in Acapulco when

I was filming on location. One morning I had the day off and was playing paddle tennis with Placido Domingo at his house when news reached me that my son Geoffrey had been born. There was much celebrating and Placido said, 'Let me film a personal message for the boy'. Of course, I never bothered trying to assemble the tapes or have them transferred to DVD, and now they just sit there gathering dust.

I'd have loved to have my own Q Branch
at home to develop gadgets.
(© 1962-2017 Danjaq LLC and United Artists Corp.)

In the Bond films we had Q to supply the latest gadgets and gizmos, many of which were actually prototypes of real designs and are now in everyday use. But, I ask myself, would Q have come up with something as deeply frustrating as the self-service till?

My mother always used to say, 'The older you get, the better you get, unless you're a banana'.

BETTY WHITE

Shops used to have a row of smiling cashiers waiting and willing to help you make a purchase. Now there are banks of soulless machines that scan your items and supposedly make the whole shopping experience easier and quicker. Oh yes?

Have you ever placed your basket of groceries down and started scanning them only for the thing to start getting agitated and flashing up hieroglyphics with accompanying messages such as my personal favourite, 'unexpected item in bagging area'? Tell me about it!

At first you can't help but look around, sheepishly and

feeling quite guilty, until one of the former cashiers – now relegated to a back room somewhere – sees the situation and comes to your aid. They explain it was because you eagerly scanned two items in succession and didn't allow the necessary 'bit of time' in between. So you get free lessons in check-out skills before being left to continue. But wait! The lights start up again! You have picked an age-restricted item, anything from a bottle of wine to a box of matches. Thankfully the former cashier appears again to vouch that you are indeed over twenty-one.

'Have you used any of our bags?' it asks. Obviously not, as I selected 'I have my own bag with me' when I first approached the machine.

'Please swipe your loyalty card.'

'I don't have one,' I press.

'Would you like a loyalty card?'

'No, I wouldn't.'

'Are you sure you wouldn't like a loyalty card?'

'No!' I confirm.

'If you take out a loyalty card today we'll give you 0.00000001 per cent off your next purchase!'

'I still don't want one.'

'Are you collecting vouchers for schools?' it asks.

'No,' I choose.

'Would you like to start collecting vouchers for schools?'

'No,' I confirm again.

'Insert your payment.'

I stick in my credit card only to be told there's a problem and this till has now reverted to 'cash only' and I should go to another till.

Better still, have you tried buying a newspaper at the airport? Not only do you have to go through all of the above but you have to scan your boarding card too. When I say, 'It's with my wife, and she has gone ahead to the bookshop,' they just look at me, smiling in their own helpful way.

Just who do these tills make the shopping experience easier for?

If you go into a large bank, you'll likely find – again – that most of the serving positions have now been replaced by machines.

'The machines can do anything a cashier can,' you're proudly told by a young person hopping around with an iPad clutched in hand.

'I have an old £50 note I found in a jacket and would like to exchange it for a new one,' I said during such an encounter a little while back.

'Ah,' replied the hopping person, 'if you log into your account and pay it through the machine, you can then withdraw fifty pounds in new notes.'

Twenty minutes later, old £50 still clamped in palm, I'm wondering what happened to cashiers who could just serve you?

Kristina recently ventured into a bank in Switzerland to draw some cash from the ATM. It was one of those all-singing all-dancing models that had so many options, buttons, slots and lights that Kristina didn't quite know how to get started.

'Could you help me?' she asked a staff member, whose job, it appeared, was to try and avoid all customers at all costs.

'I need to draw some cash,' Kristina continued, proffering her bank card, 'but I'm not quite sure ...'

'Do you bank with us Madame?' he asked, helpfully.

'No, I just want to use the ATM.'

'If you don't bank with us, I am not at liberty to help you use the ATM,' he concluded, before walking off.

I know what you're thinking – Swiss bankers!

Have you bought something – anything – electrical recently? Once upon a time there used to be an instruction booklet that came with the item. Admittedly it was written in fifteen different languages and typeset in the tiniest of print, but at least you had something to refer to. Nowadays there's nothing other than a flyer with a website address to download instructions and register for a warranty. So, when I bought a new toaster recently, I was given a web address. That's fine, only the address doesn't seem to work, or at least the page I need won't load up.

How difficult can it be, you ask, to use a toaster? Back in the days when there was one knob and one slide-down button, it was a piece of cake (or toast), but this one requires you to set temperatures, timings, desired colourings and all that jazz.

When I do manage to log into an online instruction manual, I've found – and this is a prime example of Sod's Law – I either end up with 130 pages in multiple languages, which start auto-printing, or a single page appertaining to the next model up to the one I bought, so it makes little or no sense at all.

It may sound alien to younger readers, but when one used to check into hotels the receptionist would give you a key. Yes, a metal key on a keyring, which unlocked and locked the room door and which you left with reception when you went out, enabling them, in the case of an emergency, to quickly check who was in and who was out.

WHAT IF ...?

My Own Chat Show

I made a couple of appearances – on 25 October and 19 December 1969 – on *Dee Time*, a chat show hosted by Simon Dee on the BBC, to talk about my life and career. I must have made quite an impression with Tom Sloan (the then head of BBC light entertainment) as when, a few weeks later, Dee moved across to ITV, I was offered my own chat show. It was to have run for thirteen weeks and I made a comment to the press: 'The BBC bent over backwards to get me and offered a great deal of money.'

Having thought about it though, I turned it down, explaining: 'The series would not have interfered with my other work. I turned it down because I am essentially an actor and when I act I use only a tiny part of my own personality. A TV show is much more demanding, particularly if you are to appear as only yourself throughout.'

Then some bright spark came up with the idea of doing away with keys in favour of swipe cards – magnetic swipe cards that could be re-used (as could keys, I hasten to add, but no one was listening to me).

So, I ask you, how many times have you stayed in a top floor room, at the furthest end of the corridor from the lift, only to discover your swipe card has been 'demagnetized' and you need to trek back down to reception?

'Don't put it near your mobile phone,' they helpfully suggest. I *didn't*.

It seems that some of those security sensors you find at the entrance to shops have a habit of affecting the magnetization, so pass through a few shop doors and you've had it!

These same swipe cards have to be inserted into a little slot on the wall just inside the room, which then activates the lights, heating and all other electrical devices in green-conscious establishments. Great idea, yes? Well, not when you want to leave your laptop or phone to charge while you go down to dinner, and not when you intend to leave on the extra electric heaters they've just brought up to the room because it was so freezing cold when you arrived. After dinner, you return only to find a) your device hasn't charged up, and b) the heaters weren't on. Why? *Because you removed the card from the slot and took it downstairs with you, which means all power is cut!* Why did you do that? *Because you needed to be able to get back into the room, of course!*

Please offer this seat to an old fart.

The other thing I've found with hotels is that they don't offer wake-up calls whereby someone at reception will actually pick up a phone, call your room and stay on the line until you pick up and say, 'OK, OK! I'm up!' No, they suggest you go into the TV menu and flick through various pages of welcome notes and adverts until you reach the alarm-setting option. Of course, this relies on the TV having been set up with the correct time in the first place.

Many's the time I've been awoken with a jolt at 5 a.m. when the TV switches itself on two hours ahead of schedule.

Excuse me as I unclench my jaw …

I find crosswords and puzzles are a great way of keeping the mind sharp and giving one a little light relief from the strains and tensions of the day. I had a lovely line in a film I made back in 1980 called *North Sea Hijack*. James Mason played Admiral Brinsden and was rather aghast at ffolkes' (that was me, with two small fs) rather unorthodox approach to things, and he also seemed to dislike my character being a bit of a know-it-all.

'I suppose you're one of those fellows who does *The Times* crossword puzzle in ten minutes?' says Brinsden.

'I have *never* taken TEN minutes,' replies ffolkes.

I do have my favourite crosswords to tackle, though I never time myself – that would be simply too gauche.

Keeping the mind sharp is indeed all-important as you get older, and reading is another big love of my life. Having waded my way through many scripts in my career – the rejected pile being bigger than the accepted ones – I've always had something on the bedside table to study, and that's why I always have to have a book on the go.

WHAT IF ...?

Escape to Victory (1981)

In 1981 I was approached by director Brian Hutton (*Where Eagles Dare*) about starring in this film. The thing is, I can't run, and to be on a field of professional football players and look convincing was something I had terrible apprehensions about. I told myself: 'I'm an actor, I can do anything.' But thinking for another minute or two, I then told myself, 'Actually, no, Rog. Steady on!'

I very nearly believed myself for a moment. Perish that thought.

In the event, John Huston went on to direct Michael Caine and Sylvester Stallone in the lead cast. Just think, I could have gone on to be Rocky!

Being a gadget nut, I ordered a Kindle as soon as they came out. The idea of being able to store hundreds – even thousands – of books on one device that I could take with me all over the world was very appealing. But you know what? I never really got on with it. I much prefer to hold a book in my hand. There's just something about turning the pages – also, we authors earn more from printed copies!

My preference is for thrillers, and I particularly like the Nordic writer Jo Nesbø and the Harry Hole thrillers. James Clavell was another great favourite. Incidentally, I worked with his daughter, the actress Michaela Clavell, when she played Miss Moneypenny's assistant Penelope Smallbone in *Octopussy* – I like to toss these little nuggets to you now and then.

Breaking bread with *Breaking Bad* star Bryan Cranston.

I also enjoy autobiographies and biographies, probably because I'm nosey. Do I flick to the index to see if I'm mentioned? Never. Well, hardly ever. One of the best I read recently was Bryan Cranston's memoir *A Life in Parts*; I met him backstage at a TV show in London, when we were in adjacent dressing rooms. A year or two before, Michael Caine had given me a box set of *Breaking Bad* for Christmas and I absolutely loved it, so I was delighted to be able to tell Bryan. He was genuinely surprised and pleased – and very chatty. I liked him, so I thought I'd buy his book – hilarious. Maybe he'll return the favour?

With advancing age you'll find it's also useful to rest your brain during the day; that is to say take a little nap – sometime after lunch and before dinner seems optimal. Admittedly it's not always voluntary and I find it often coincides with me putting on a DVD and sitting down with an ice cream. I remember the first thirty minutes of the film vividly, but the middle is just a blank.

Which simply means that DVDs last all the longer in our house.

I couldn't play as well as my dad, but boy did I look cool!

THINGS THAT
ANNOY ME

I've written about things that have impressed me over my lifetime, and the great advances we've made in science and technology, but I do honestly worry that overall standards have dropped in society. Good manners, I was always told, cost nothing, yet they seem to be slipping in modern life. If you asked a young man these days why he should walk on the outside when with a lady, would he know? If you told someone it is polite to hold a door open, would they agree? Do people actually say 'please' and 'thank you' to others?

Do men ever stand up when a lady enters the room?

There seems to be a more casual attitude nowadays, which in its place is fine, but why don't prime ministers and senior politicians wear ties and suits like they used to? Why do people think it's acceptable to turn up at the theatre with their backsides hanging out of their torn jeans? I remember dressing up to go to the local cinema, or at least making an effort to look smart. And take a look at the photograph opposite – a suit and tie to bang out a few chords on the guitar? You bet!

The 1960s certainly brought about more relaxed and laid-back attitudes, but directors on film sets would still wear suits and ties. People in authority and public office set an example. Now you'll likely see more of them in T-shirts and shorts than you will in a shirt and tie. The one exception seems to be male TV newsreaders and weather presenters. They're almost always immaculately turned out with suits and smart ties and I think it sets a very professional tone and standard.

In my younger days, men always wore hats too and if you were ever on a bus passing the Cenotaph in Whitehall, they all made a point of raising their hats, as they would when passing hearses. It was an expression of good manners and eternal thanks. I stirred things up in 2016 when the new series of TV's *Top Gear* filmed fast cars doing stunts around the Cenotaph. I thought it was disgraceful and showed a total lack of respect, and said as much. Of course, the usual social media trolls called me all sorts of names and said I was an outdated old fart (or words to that effect), which only saddened me more.

But maybe I'm old-fashioned now?

Eating in theatres, cinemas, art galleries and on public transport is commonplace. I'm not just talking about a sandwich or an ice cream either, I'm talking about smelly, noisy meals and takeaway coffees and soups. Certain members of the audience sitting in the front row think nothing of putting their drinks and their feet on the edge of the stage as though it's the table in their lounge.

People seem to treat the theatre as though they are at home watching the television. As so many people don't eat at a dining table any more, in favour of eating and drinking in front of the box while simultaneously chatting, texting, tweeting, checking emails and shopping online, they think it's OK to do similar when watching a play or film. I suppose it's 'the age of entitlement'?

WHAT IF ...?

Dallas

In 1986, *Dallas* was at its popular height and the producers made overtones to my agent about me appearing in eight episodes as 'a British tycoon who has a showdown with JR.' It sounded intriguing and as it was one of the highest rated TV shows at the time, I was interested to know more. I never saw a script though, and as I still hadn't officially resigned from the role of 007, maybe they were worried another Bond film was in the offing? Anyhow, nothing came of it and JR went on to have other sparring partners throughout the rest of its run.

And why, please tell, do people in towns and cities walk around while devouring pies, pasties and sandwiches in one hand with takeaway drinks in the other, as they rush along? Are they too hungry to wait to get back to their desks, or too busy to stop, sit down and enjoy a few minutes on a bench?

Something else that never fails to raise my hackles is when you watch a great television show and the end credits are squeezed. When actors or technicians work on a TV show, they are always credited at the end. In fact a lot of them pick up their next job because they were spotted in a particularly good role or on a great show by a casting director or a producer. But a few years ago, the credits started being squeezed into a corner of the screen (making them totally unreadable) to allow a trailer for 'what's coming next' or 'coming next week' to play out in the remainder of the screen, often with an annoying voiceover.

Research by the actors' union Equity found that, of the 10,000 respondents, the vast majority detested credits being diminished in this way. They complained that the practice ruins their viewing experience and prompts them to switch channels. So it hardly does the desired trick of keeping viewers for the following programme.

The BBC promised to curb its credit-squeezing habits, but it will not be stopping it altogether and instead vowed to make sure the credits run in full for at least one episode of a drama or comedy. Besides which, they helpfully pointed out, viewers could always go online to look them up if they were that bothered.

Huh!

Language is another bugbear of mine and I don't mean swearing – I admit, the odd cuss word such as 'drat' or 'damn' has passed my lips over the years. I mean this dreadful slang and text language that has crept in to everyday life, such as 'Sup?' as a form of greeting, 'Laters' as a form of goodbye, 'YOLO' (You Only Live Once), 'AMA' (ask me anything) and so on and on.

Yes, we still have cockney rhyming slang that originated in the East End of London – 'apples and pears', 'trouble and strife', 'plates of meat' – which some say came out of a sense of community, or perhaps market traders talking among themselves in such a way that customers would not know what they were talking about. Or was it developed by criminals to confuse the police? Whatever its origin, it was used by a relative minority. Nowadays, however, it's commonplace to hear slang everywhere and it's really quite bemusing. For example, not so long ago, when someone said they were 'sick', you would know they'd be in bed with a pimpled glass bottle of Lucozade in an orange crinkly cellophane wrapper. Now we're supposed to know that 'sick' means 'great' as in, 'That's well sick, mate.'

I was a little taken aback when someone described me as 'FAF' last year. I'd always thought things that were a 'faff' were a bit of a pain. Oh no, this 'FAF', I discovered, was a

107

supposed compliment, though I'll leave you to look it up!

The English language seems to have become very informal and lazy, and I find it rather sad. To overhear youngsters talk nowadays is quite baffling, and I wonder, when they go for a job interview, if 'All right there, mate?' is going to be a suitable enough greeting, and if 'Yeah, whatever, bruvva', would be a means of agreeing to accept the job?

In their own shorthand, it is 'so not amaze', 'so not incred' ... but it is 'so ridic'.

WHAT IF ...?

Home Alone 2: Lost in New York (1992)

I was invited to meet with child actor Macaulay Culkin in Chicago to discuss the sequel to his star-making vehicle. He had the final say over casting – aged twelve! – but I believe script and character changes followed, so it wasn't to be.

Who knows? I could have had a new career as a screen baddie in a string of children's films.

In wanting to blend in, and be up with the kids (or is it down?), I thought it appropriate to reveal the old folks' text shorthand:

ATD – At the doctors

BTW – Bring the wheelchair

BYOT – Bring your own teeth

FWIW – Forgot where I was

IMHO – Is my hearing aid on?

GGPBL – Gotta go, pacemaker battery low

ROFLACGU – Rolling on floor laughing and can't get up

TTYL – Talk to you louder

Anyhow, whatevs, LOL.

I communicate a lot by email and text and I also tweet away on Twitter – I really am up/down with the kids. However, Kristina sometimes gets a little frustrated when I'm in my study on my computer for long periods, as she thinks it's a bit unsociable. I understand what she means, as there's nothing worse than trying to have a conversation with someone who is preoccupied tapping away on a keyboard or tablet.

It could, on occasion, be termed 'unsocial media' and it's something we need to be wary of. When children stop interacting with conversations and turn to their phones and tablets to text instead; when families don't sit down for a meal together any longer and chat – even if it's only about the latest games they bought; when people are unable to put their phones away for a couple of hours in a cinema ... I fear for future generations who don't have the chance to develop conversational skills.

And apart from conversational skills, I read an interesting article the other day that proposed that handwriting skills were deteriorating as more people use digital media to communicate – texting and typing being increasingly used over penmanship. What will happen to the dear old handwritten letter? Again, sorry to sound like an old fart, but I love receiving letters from family and fans. That someone has sat down and thoughtfully composed a few lines just for me, well, it gives me a warm and fuzzy feeling. It's important that we don't lose ourselves in the technology we've created.

I know my grandchildren laugh when I talk about the days before mobile phones. To think most households had just one wired-in phone in their hallway, and how calls were much cheaper in the evenings and to local numbers. Others without a phone at home relied on the local phone box, where you'd often have to queue to use it. You had to book a transatlantic call and wait an hour or more for it to be connected – at huge expense, and with a fairly poor line.

Back when the world was in black and white and standard definition, we survived OK.

There were even times on film sets when I remember we used to drop a white handkerchief to signal to the crew or artists in the distance that cameras were rolling – imagine that!

Of course now every phone has a camera and I remember Prince Charles bemoaning the fact that every arm seems to have a camera at the end of it nowadays; but do people actually print their photographs? I have albums and boxes full of snaps at home, but must admit since I started snapping on my phone (I'm just as guilty!) I hardly ever have prints made. What do you do when you change your phone though? I know the cloud is up there, but long gone are the days when you'd send a film off to be processed and await the return of the envelope – often with other people's photos mixed in. In the days of Facebook and Instagram I suppose they're there, floating around in the ether, but I still like the feel of holding prints in my hand.

Talking of old farts (me, you understand, not Prince Charles) some kind soul sent me this recently. Now, I'm pretty sure it has nothing to do with Harvard School of Psychiatry, and I have no idea who devised it, but see what you think.

Harvard University
Mental Age Assessment

The following was developed as a mental age assessment by the School of Psychiatry at Harvard University. Take your time and see if you can read each line aloud without a mistake.

The average person over sixty years of age cannot do it!

1. This is this cat.

2. This is is cat.

3. This is how cat.

4. This is to cat.

5. This is keep cat

6. This is an cat.

7. This is old cat.

8. This is fart cat.

9. This is busy cat.

10. This is for cat.

11. This is forty cat.

12. This is seconds cat.

Now go back and read the third word in each line from the top down.

It did make me laugh but, really, the world wide web, what is it coming to?

Having grown up in the war years, I was always wary of wasting or throwing anything away. Socks and pullovers were darned when they first went into holes, boots were mended and coats were patched up. It wasn't only a money issue that made us so frugal; we were also abiding by the watchwords of 'Make Do and Mend', as in the pamphlet issued by the British Ministry of Information, which was intended to provide families with useful tips on how to be both frugal and stylish in times of harsh rationing.

Readers were advised to create pretty 'decorative patches' to cover holes in worn garments; unpick old jumpers to re-knit alternatives; turn men's clothes into women's; as well as how to protect against the 'moth menace'.

Make do and mend.

My father was a dab hand at DIY and could pretty much fix anything from a wonky shelf to a radio to a cup handle that had broken. My mother could sew and repair garments brilliantly. There was no disposable plastic packaging; milk came in bottles, which were washed and reused, and loose foods were parcelled up in paper bags and boxes. My mother had a string shopping bag that she always took out with her, as there were no carrier bags on offer.

But after the war things changed. People were understandably fed up of 'making do' and being penny-wise; they wanted to splash out on new clothes and luxury goods such as refrigerators, televisions and the like – albeit it on HP or rental. Only ten years later, in August 1955, *Life* magazine ran a story called 'Throwaway Living', which warned of the changing approach society was taking to everyday goods. In more recent times we've been accustomed to recycling and the importance of cutting down on plastic shopping bags, which are a total menace to landfill sites, but we have also, conversely, become a throwaway society. I'm not saying we should start darning socks again, but how many times have you heard the phrase, 'Throw it away, it's cheaper to buy a new one'?

My mother could never bear to see food wasted, and I still dutifully try to clear my plates at meals, but when I hear that up to forty per cent of edible food is thrown away, it makes me shudder. Maybe we need a lesson in consumerism?

I find it rather sad that society has become so blasé in its attitudes of just tossing things in the bin – and it's an attitude that risks extending far and above household items and food, too.

Coffee used to come with two choices: black or white. In Italy and Italian coffee bars around the world, you could get a nice strong espresso to start off your morning, or perhaps a cappuccino to ease in to the day with a little less

Make mine a tall non-fat latte with a caramel drizzle, please.

of a caffeine kick. Now, however, when you enter a coffee shop you're presented with a menu of baffling proportions and can't simply ask for 'a coffee'. I scan the board and find myself wondering whether a decaf soya milk latte actually tastes like coffee? What is an ice burnt caramel latte? A salted toffee macadamia latte anyone? A piccino? And who dreamt up caffe misto? Dare I even think about a Java chip frappucino? Is caffe mocha coffee, or a hot chocolate with an identity crisis? And why on earth are they all served in soup bowls with two handles? Who can drink that much coffee?

Then there are smoothies (we used to call them milkshakes in my day), and teas from all over the world … leaving me totally perplexed as to what to ask for, not to say blooming annoyed!

There are at least two things on this table that I can no longer enjoy – but the flower is nice.

THINGS THEY NEVER TELL YOU TO EXPECT

R eaching eighty-nine is rather lovely, though on the flip side, attaining this great age doesn't come without its own issues. Actress Miriam Margoyles recently said, 'No one tells you old age is going to be shitty.' Perhaps a little indelicately put, but nonetheless perceptive.

Playing secret heroes, action-adventure characters and suave crime stoppers was all in a day's work for me as a young, agile actor. Yes, back then I could leap out of cars, run up stairs without taking a breath and happily throw myself around sets for fight sequences, often without putting a hair on my well-lacquered head out of place.

Ah, in those heady days I enjoyed sumptuous lunches made from the most extravagant and finest ingredients, not to mention the very best champagnes and wines to complement the meal, followed by decadent desserts.

Well, mate, that's all stopped!

I now glare at stairs with contempt and huge suspicion. Instead of leaping out, I have to prise myself carefully from cars while desperately trying not to accidentally break wind in the driver's face. Oh, and the only thing I seem able to fight with is my seemingly hermetically sealed glasses case while trying to get my reading specs out to study a menu – hoping to find more simple foods that don't give me indigestion or heartburn.

If you worry, you die. If you don't worry, you also die. So why worry?

MIKE HORN

WHAT IF ...?

Vendetta (c. 1993)

In 1993 the TV movie *Barbarians at the Gate*, based on a book by Bryan Burrough, was produced, with James Garner in the lead. It was both a critical and commercial success. In subsequent interviews Burrough mentioned his other book, *Vendetta*, which was centred around the American Express takeover of a private bank run by Edmond Safra. After a bitter dispute, the $450 million takeover was later reversed and Edmond won a public apology from American Express for starting a smear campaign against him, plus $8 million in damages, all of which he donated to charities.

There was talk of making a movie of this book, with me playing the chairman of American Express, however, the project never materialized.

Six years later, in December 1999, Edmond Safra and his nurse Vivian Torrente were suffocated by fumes in a fire that was deliberately lit at the billionaire's Monaco home by another of his carers, in a bizarre attempt for the arsonist to gain more recognition from his employer. It was a huge tragedy.

In 2013, my doctor declared, 'You have type two diabetes.' Mind you, I wasn't terribly surprised, given that I had recently collapsed on the sofa with an unquenchable thirst.

'So what does that mean?' I enquired, hoping the answer would be 'not too much'. I didn't want anything to rock my routine.

'No booze, no puddings, no chocolate, no sugar,' said the doc. Was that a hint of glee I saw in his eyes?

For someone who liked all four – sometimes, I admit, to excess – it was a rather deflating moment when I was proffered a diet sheet at the hospital. I remember seeing such delicious, saliva-inducing foods as 'plain brown boiled rice' and 'unsweetened wholegrain cereals' on the list. I frantically scanned down the page looking for my beloved baked beans on toast. No! Apparently there is 'too much sugar' in them, and those delicious toasted baguettes I enjoyed with lots of butter contain 'refined carbohydrates'; it had to be wholemeal bread from now on. Furthermore, there was to be no full-fat dairy or cream (bang went the butter), fruit juice, fatty cuts of meat – surely that doesn't include pork pies? – or fried foods. Could I still enjoy the occasional ginger beer shandy? Afraid not. I had to watch my weight, my cholesterol and my sugar intake. If I didn't, I'd potentially risk everything from foot damage

My favourite tipple (non-alcoholic, of course).

(including possible amputation) to heart disease – just what a hypochondriac needs to hear.

To be serious for a moment, it was certainly a wake-up call and I immediately felt guilty for all those years of stuffing my face; though my doctor assured me that age was also a contributing factor to the condition. Oh no, another downside to getting older! Though I should add the condition doesn't just strike old folks, as my friend Tom Hanks revealed in 2013. He was only in his mid fifties when he was diagnosed with diabetes and blamed not following a healthier diet when he was younger. Let that be a warning to you, dear reader – eat and live healthily as you only have one body.

I now take a daily pill, measure my blood sugar regularly and dutifully record the results, though occasionally I wonder if my readings are a bit too high or a bit too low?

Nevertheless they're beautifully written up. And when I say 'no chocolate', I should admit I soon discovered diabetic-friendly bars. That was a momentous day and I was a total pig. If only I had managed to open up my glasses case when I made that all-important initial purchase I'd have read the label that stated 'Consumed in any quantity, they act as a laxative' …

Speaking of visiting the smallest room in the house, when I turned eighty I was warned to ensure that I always zipped up after using the facilities, as apparently some men forget. That's not so much a problem for me nowadays … as long as I'm reminded to zip down first. One of later life's worries is definitely having a keener interest in knowing where the loos are situated. You too may hear yourself saying, 'Ought I to pop in – just in case?'

In forever seeking the elixir of youth my ears pricked up when someone, somewhere, said that beetroot juice is good for you. It supposedly helps lower high blood pressure and prevents dementia. As I had a touch of the former and was keen to ward off the latter, I bought a couple of litre bottles and happily drank them throughout the course of a day. As I gulped it all down I kept thinking how this quite sour detox drink would be doing me no end of good inside; that is until I discovered beetroot juice, served in any great quantity,

WHAT IF ...?

The Specialist (1994)

Sylvester Stallone – with whom I very nearly appeared in *Escape to Victory* – and Sharon Stone were being lined up for this all-action Paramount Pictures production, and I was approached about starring (with options on sequels) but at the time I was seeing my own specialists about prostate cancer and couldn't commit to the movie, nor would I have imagined the insurance companies would have sanctioned my casting with ongoing treatment taking place.

Maybe it was fortuitous, as I don't think it would have done me any favours. Reviewers were pretty scathing. Roger Ebert said: '*The Specialist* is one of those films that forces the characters through torturous mazes of dialogue and action, to explain a plot that is so unlikely it's not worth the effort. You know a movie's in trouble when the people in line at the parking garage afterward are trying to figure out what the heroine's motivations were.'

is also the most wonderful and effective laxative. My gut has rarely been more mobile, if you'll forgive the turn of phrase, forcing me to retire with some haste – again! – to the smallest room, where, some time later, I noticed our once white bathroom suite had turned a very garish shade of pink.

There have been certain foods I've avoided most of my life – strawberries and coriander being two prime examples. I just don't like them. Cucumbers, on the other hand, always seemed to be fairly innocent fruits (or are they a vegetable? No, I'm sure they're a fruit) mixed in with salads and shredded to accompany crispy duck, pancakes and hoisin sauce. So whoever would have thought innocent old cucumbers would turn on me in later life? Now they must be avoided for fear of triggering involuntary exhalations. Yes, that green gas-inducing fiend has a lot to answer for.

Enough talk of laxatives and wind!

'What's that?' you say. Oh dear, have you gone a bit mutt and jeff?

Well, Kristina will sympathize, as she grew quite fed up of me asking her, 'What was that?' almost every time she spoke to me. That and her walking into the television room to find the walls vibrating because of the excessive volume, only to find me having an oblivious snooze, pointed to one thing: yes folks, the old hearing wasn't what it once was.

The same happened with my father and I bought him a hearing device that could be best described as a small radio-sized box with a wired earpiece. Quite often he would forget to switch it on – you could always tell, as, in trying to hear what he himself was saying, he'd be virtually shouting across a restaurant tab!

❧

As we grow older, we must discipline ourselves to continue expanding, broadening, learning, keeping our minds active and open.

CLINT EASTWOOD

❧

Of course, technology has advanced hugely and everything has shrunk in size, so when it came to my turn I was able to buy some very nifty, almost invisible, tiny little hearing aids, which slip effortlessly into both ears and which are on continually. Well, until their batteries run out.

The only trouble then is that I can't see the damn things to change the batteries (the 'virtually invisible' slogan is certainly accurate). Once I get my glasses case open and lay out the devices and the tiny pinhead-sized batteries on my

WHAT IF ...?

The Red Phone (1996)

In August 1996, *The Globe* reported that I was set to sign a $6 million deal for four TV movies, as the head of a *Mission: Impossible*-type team battling terrorists around the world. Called *The Red Phone* the story continued: 'Industry experts predict the flicks will be a big hit in the light of the deadly TWA Flight 800 tragedy and the terrorist bombing at the Atlanta Olympics. These films will air as television movies in the US, but will be released as feature films in Europe, a source explains. In addition to his hefty salary, Roger will share a percentage of earnings from the theatre releases and video sales.'

If only these industry experts actually knew what they were talking about! I never saw $6 let alone $6 million, nor a script.

desk, I find I often accidentally knock one onto the floor. Kristina will join me on my hands and knees peering and shuffling around trying to find the proverbial needle in a haystack.

Fairly recently, on leaving a theatre dressing room, I unhooked the cheek microphone I'd been using on stage, dashed out to the car and off to our hotel a few miles away to have my late evening tea and toast while watching the news. The TV was obviously faulty though, as it was only producing sound from the speaker on the left-hand side – and even that sounded a bit muted. That's when I realized I must have flicked my right-ear hearing aid out when I removed the cheek mic. We were leaving at eight o'clock the next morning for the next venue, a three-hour drive away, and so at 11 p.m. we made the mad dash back to the theatre, arriving just as the stage door keeper was locking up. A joint hands-and-knees effort found the offending gadget in the dressing-room shag pile. Phew!

And why is it that I can guarantee those batteries that I spend an hour replacing will always run down when I'm either giving a speech, on stage or taking part in a TV interview? As they run out of juice, they 'helpfully' emit a repeated and ever-louder 'da-da-da-da' noise, which, of course, only I can hear. No one told me this when I bought them, so many was the time I thought a loud radio had been switched on behind me. To say it's a distraction is an understatement and you may just see me on a TV show looking longingly over the host's shoulder – not at anyone in particular, but rather in the hope they'll go to a commercial break so as I can dash off and remove the orchestra in my ear.

You can't help getting older, but you can help yourself from becoming old and infirm, in mind as well as body.

JOAN COLLINS

Worse still, I often forget to put them in and have undoubtedly left many TV hosts quite perplexed as to why I answer questions they never quite asked me. Then again, perhaps they shouldn't mumble!

As hearing goes a little awry with advancing age, so does eyesight. Admittedly I've worn glasses for several decades, and contact lenses when filming, which, of course, are as fiddly as heck to fit and often leave me with tears running down my cheeks.

At some point, if you live long enough, you'll hear the immortal words: 'You do have a cataract, but it's not ripe yet,' from an ophthalmic optician with an almost euphoric sense of anticipation.

So, faculties start failing; what else goes wrong? Well, hair grows everywhere you don't want it to, and not where it should: it's a bit much when my barber spends more time trimming my ears than my fringe. Oh yes, there's lots of fun to look forward to!

As you grow older, you'll likely notice an unpleasant side-effect of the process: you can't handle hangovers as well as you used to. Or am I just imagining they get worse with advancing years? Although my boozing days are now behind me, there was once a time when, after a heavy night on the Jack Daniels, I could laugh off a hangover and report for work fresh-faced and raring to go. In later years, though, the day after the night before would start a little quieter and a little more slowly.

The dry mouth. The nausea. The fatigue. The feeling that your head is going to drop off. Yes! That all gets worse and there is medical research to back me up on this. Scientists have discovered that the older one gets the less efficient the body becomes at breaking down alcohol. Apparently there's a chemical in the body called acetaldehyde, which is the thing responsible for those headaches and the feelings of nausea, and because we all gain fat as we get older and fat can't absorb alcohol, that means there's less space for it to diffuse.

Also, they say another reason why hangovers get worse is due to a decrease in body water content, which leaves concentrated alcohol in your system for longer. So take a tip from me: drink lots of water after a boozy night out!

Do you like sport? Getting socks on is now a two-person Olympic sport in our house and, much like a tug of war, I pull and Kristina pushes. We jiggle and we twist until, eventually … success. Only then do I find that my ankles have swollen in the Monaco summer heat so I can't get my bloody shoes on. I'm sure it's not the done thing to turn up at formal occasions wearing tennis shoes but then again people are so busy staring at my ear hair that it doesn't really notice.

Besides, I don't dress for fashion, I dress for comfort. My preferred mode of attire is a blazer and grey slacks. I asked my tailor if double-breasted jackets are in vogue, 'No, but they will be once they see you in this one,' said the silver-tongued outfitter. Though, as Kristina says, you can really

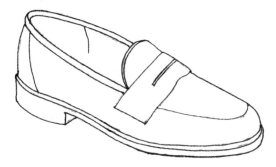

The slip-on shoe – a delight after wrestling with one's socks.

attend any function dressed in a good blazer: from lunch to a garden party, a film preview to a swanky dinner out, it's multi-functional.

As you get older, your immune system isn't quite as strong so you are a bit more susceptible to coughs and colds – well, I've certainly found that. They're not spread as much through the air as they are through hand contact. Yes, if you shake hands with someone you're more likely to pick up their germs! Pushing trolleys around a food store or carrying a shopping basket around is just as treacherous. So we carry a little bottle of hand gel with us and when we walk into a shop or a restaurant or a building, after shaking hands with several people – anyone who proffers a limb

– we discreetly take a little gel and rub our hands. It's at this point you can always guarantee someone who wasn't there a moment ago suddenly appears. They first clear their throat (into their hand) or perhaps wipe their nose moving that glistening dew drop into their palm, before offering the

WHAT IF ...?

Love Letters (1996)

Having not appeared in front of audience on a theatre stage for approaching five decades, I appeared on the *Clive Anderson All Talk* chat show in 1996 and mentioned that an offer had been made for me to make a return to the theatre with a new rendition of A.R. Gurney's *Love Letters*, co-starring my old friend Joan Collins.

The producers didn't get it together, however, until four years later, and I was off doing other things. Typical. Joan, meanwhile, hit it off with tour manager Percy Gibson, and they married in 2002. I was there at the wedding!

sweatiest of excited hands and pressing it into yours. They then insist on gripping it firmly as they relate a long story to you. You can almost feel the germs penetrating.

The French have it right when they kiss on the cheeks – far more healthy. I should explain this is not to be referred to as 'French kissing'. That's quite different and we won't go there.

With all these bits of the body beginning to show signs of wear, that leads me to the subject of my proctologist – no, I jest. It's not all doom and gloom and there are actually some upsides to ageing and some may just prove useful:

- You perspire less. It's something to do with the sweat glands shrinking. I can't possibly comment on other glands shrinking, however.
- Your teeth are less sensitive. That's not because you have more implants than teeth; no, over time you accumulate more dentin (hard tissue) between the outer enamel of a tooth and its central nerve. So you can enjoy more ice cream, for instance, without shooting pains firing all across your mouth.

No comment.

- You have less taste. Not sartorially, though I do wonder at some people, but because you lose some of your taste buds. So basically, you're quite happy to eat anything and think it tastes OK. You'll please even the most mediocre of cooks.
- You are happier. This is true. I certainly became more content with the passing of time. Once you pass the nadir of middle age, things start looking up and you have time to do the things you want to now you're not rushing around trying to support a family.
- You can get into cinemas, theatres, galleries and other places cheaper.
- You'll also find people willing to give up their seats for you, though I've yet to see if that works in the theatre or at a concert where I'd like a better position.
- If you forget something, or someone's name, you

134

can explain it away as a 'senior moment' and you'll discover people are very forgiving.

- Meanwhile, and not a lot of people know this (who was it who said that?), our feet become longer and wider with age. It's something to do with tendons and ligaments losing elasticity, which in turn allows the toes to spread out and the arch of the foot to flatten. Some people can gain as much as one shoe size every ten years – and you know what they say about big feet!

Being older and hopefully a little wiser also means you're more confident in making decisions, and you feel more qualified to make your thoughts known. That isn't to say people will choose to listen. It's also interesting that your relationship with your children changes too. We've all been there through the teenage years I'm sure, when nothing you say or do is fair and in fact you probably embarrass your children more than anything else.

'Please don't meet me outside the school.'

'No, I'd rather walk, thanks.'

'Oh, do you have to come with me?'

These are all familiar statements. But as you grow older so do your children, and when they in turn have their own

My children, Christian, Deborah and Geoffrey,
drawn by me in 1977.

offspring it's reassuring to know they suddenly 'get it' – they understand you and perhaps even appreciate you more. In short, your relationship changes and you become closer. In fact you become friends.

I also believe that with great wisdom comes greater humility. You're not afraid to admit when you're wrong, or to stop for a moment, take a breath and see things from someone else's point of view. You also learn not to judge or criticize so much. We all make mistakes and sometimes you need to allow others the chance to make their own mistakes and not judge them – you know they'll learn from their errors.

It's also true that possessions and status symbols become less important. In fact you want less. People say they don't know what to buy an older person for a birthday or at Christmas, as they pretty much already have everything they need. So this is when the old adage, 'it's the thought that counts', becomes far more apt. I'd rather have the paperback of a great book or a recommended DVD that I know I can watch and enjoy, than an expensive trinket.

In fact, when I think about it, although I know we all grumble about getting older, you are indeed thankful for being *able* to grow old. Not everyone does and many die before their time. With age comes gratitude and the knowledge that with every passing year we are blessed.

The lovely Laura Tarrant in our Swisscom advertisement.

THE WORLD OF WORK

The old adage of 'an old actor never retires, the phone just stops ringing', is absolutely true – particularly when, as in my case, you put the wrong SIM card in your mobile. Gone are the days when I can leap around shooting at villains bent on world domination, but I am fortunate in that my agent calls from time to time with the offer of a job that sounds a bit more gentle by comparison. I won't talk about the work I turn down, or the frustrating situation of having agreed to the filming dates and location for a commercial only to eventually hear that the 'client' has decided they don't want you after all. They call it 'going in another direction'. In truth they've realized they'd rather go with one of the other twelve people the advertising agency suggested in the first place. Maybe they were cheaper? Maybe they were prettier?

In early 2015, I received a very pleasant phone call from my acting agent, Jean Diamond. She said Swisscom, the Swiss telecoms company, wondered if I'd be interested in appearing in their next commercial campaign, which was filming in Zurich.

'Yeah, sure,' said I.

The whole thing moved quickly and before I knew it the shooting schedule was emailed across.

As Switzerland is largely German, Italian, French and English in its make-up, a lot of commercials are run in those different languages, and after I accepted the job I was asked if I could say a few lines in each different language. My Italian is fairly reasonable, I can get away with a sentence or two in French and, although rusty, I can string a few German words together convincingly.

Of course, that's when they got carried away and decided I should film four versions in four languages. They helpfully produced 'idiot boards' so I could glance at the lines if I got stuck!

A still from the Swisscom ad. Still raising eyebrows after all these years.

It was actually quite a witty advert, where a sales lady in the telecom store offers a special smartphone combination deal to me, but I say I don't want any special treatment and would like to be treated like any other normal customer, pointing at the lady at the counter with her back to me as an example. When the lady turns around she acts offended to be called 'normal' – she is actually a very famous Swiss model and actress, Melanie Winiger.

Anyhow, the ad runs to thirty seconds; the blooper reel is feature length!

WHAT IF ...?

Shaka Zulu (1997)

In the mid 1980s a South African mini-series was made based on the book by Joshua Sinclair about Shaka, king of the Zulu nation from 1816 to 1828, and his dealings with the British who ruled the Empire. The writer began pulling together a movie and I met with him and the director to discuss a role. Alas the financing never came together. No money, no Moore.

Between 2012 and 2016 I toured the UK each autumn, boring the pants off audiences in theatres with my 'Evening With ...' show. One of the joys of walking on to a stage and facing a live audience, for an actor at least, is feeling an instant connection. You don't get that on films or TV. It was also nice to see crowds old enough to still remember me. When it comes to audience questions, I honestly never know what might come my way. Sometimes they are quite hilarious, from, 'Did you get to shag all the Bond girls?' to a chap in Merseyside complimenting me on just about everything, only to add, 'I look at you now, admiringly. Do you know what I think when I see you immaculately turned out, knowing you can still pull the women, looking great and with a twinkle in your eye? ... Yer bastard!'

Well, you can't help but fall about laughing.

I would talk a little about UNICEF, really just scratching the surface and asking people to think about buying their greetings cards through the organization, and perhaps make a small donation in the buckets we had in the lobbies. I've always been overwhelmed and touched by their generosity. Not just on the night either, as I often received letters or

My assistant, Gareth, stands outside the theatre, scene of another 'Evening with ...'.

tweets from people afterwards saying they had set up a regular contribution to UNICEF because of the little insight I had given them at their local theatre, which made them want to go away and find out more, and help more.

Old age is like everything else. To make a success of it, you've got to start young.

THEODORE ROOSEVELT

Prior to a show in Liverpool, a man had written to me saying that his elderly mother (mind you, she was probably younger than me!) had admired me all of her life. Sadly, she had early onset dementia and, worse still, had recently been diagnosed with terminal cancer and given just a short time to live. He said it would mean so much if I would briefly meet his mother. Of course, I agreed. Kristina told me that the lady's face beamed with a massive smile as soon as she saw me.

WHAT IF ...?

The Chemical Wedding (1999-2002)

Conceived as the brainchild of Iron Maiden front man Bruce Dickinson, *The Chemical Wedding* was to be Terry Jones' (of Monty Python) new company Messiah Pictures' first production. Roger Daltrey and Malcolm McDowell were said to be heading the cast and I was also rumoured to be appearing in the film. It eventually came to fruition in 2008 with none of us rumoured people in it; in fact I was never approached.

Her son wrote to me afterwards, saying that although his mother sometimes struggled to remember who even he was, every time she looked at the photograph of us together she regaled him with the story of meeting me that night. Almost a year later, I received another letter to tell me the old lady had passed away, but that I was to be in no doubt that the brief meeting we had had boosted her life by several months. It was terribly moving and just goes to prove how taking a minute or two, showing a little kindness that you don't think of as being much at the time, can in fact have a major impact. It makes it all worthwhile.

Although the evenings were loosely structured, and we went from A to B, I would occasionally head off on tangents – particularly if I forgot what the heck I was waffling on about. But being the ever-smooth old actor, I covered it beautifully by telling a couple of jokes.

In fact, when I'm sizing up the audience, I open on the old Yiddish Theatre story ...

The curtain is late going up and, after a little commotion, the manager appears on the stage dressed in a dirty old dinner jacket that has seen far better days.

'Ladies and gentlemen,' he calls out. 'I'm afraid there will be no show tonight. I have just been in the leading lady's dressing room, and our star of the show is lying there – dead.'

A man calls out from the circle, 'Give her an enema!'

'Sir!' the manager goes on. 'You are not hearing me correctly! Our leading lady is *dead*.'

'Then give her an enema!'

'But, sir, what good would that do, as she is dead?'

'Well, it certainly can't harm!' came the response.

If I get a giggle, I carry on!

Another tactic, when I need to buy a bit of time or forget a name, is when I tell this story:

Two blokes were in a pub chatting, and the first one says, 'I've been having a bit of trouble with my ... y'know, with remembering things.'

'Oh, have you seen a doctor?' his friend asks.

'Seen a doctor about what?'

'Your memory, have you seen a doctor?'

'Oh yes.'

'Well, what did he say?' asks his mate.

'Say about what?'

'Your memory! Did he give you anything?'

'Yes, he gave me some pills.'

'What are they called?' his concerned friend enquires.

'Well, erm, oh hang on a minute ... what's the name of that little white and yellow flower that appears in the grass in summer?'

'Daisy?' he asks.

'Yes, that's it.' With that he looks over his shoulder and calls to his wife, 'Daisy, what's the name of those pills the doctor gave me?'

It usually gets a laugh and gets me back on track. You should try it!

On stage, we never quite know where our chats will take us but the audiences seem to enjoy it.

The most popular part of the evenings – well, who am I trying to kid? It's all popular! – is actually when I get on to 007. People never tire of hearing tales of Jimmy Bond. I'm often asked if I ever get fed up of it but to be so would be terribly ungrateful. I'm old enough and wise enough to appreciate the good fortune Bond brought me, and will never forget it.

WHAT IF …?

Victor (2003–2004)

In August 2003 the breaking news was that I was poised to join the cast of *Victor* (in the role of Captain Walton), which was based on a play written by Alistair Faulkner, all about the least-featured part of Mary Shelley's book, Dr Frankenstein's stay at Norsay island. They even announced that the premiere of the movie, directed by Scott Mabutt, was set for 31 October 2003. Financing matters then saw it delayed, but the producers said the good news was that I was stepping in to co-produce. Really?

I won't lie and say that driving around the country and unpacking bags for one night only at hotels isn't tiring. It is. Especially when you have an Australian driver like we do, with a satnav last updated in 1972. However, it's a wonderful way to see parts of the country that we've not enjoyed previously and also to find good pubs en route for delicious lunches.

It was while we were staying at Bray in Berkshire that we arranged a night out at the cinema. We rarely go to the cinema nowadays, preferring instead to watch new films on DVD and particularly at awards time from BAFTA and the American Academy. One exception was when *SPECTRE* was released. We couldn't make the premiere as we were on tour in Liverpool, but a few days later it hit the cinemas and

I can never resist a Bond movie at the cinema.

that coincided with a rare day off. Gareth arranged tickets at the swanky new Everyman Cinema in nearby Gerrards Cross. Of course, Kristina and I got OAP rates – after all, there's no point throwing money around.

As ever the traffic was a nightmare and we arrived just as the commercials started and slipped into our back-row seats quietly. Then the manager came in ahead of the film to welcome everyone and to remind them that there was waiter

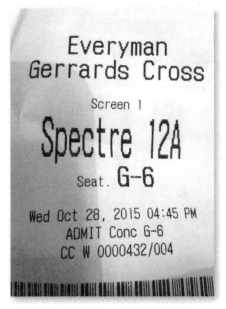

Did I mention that I keep everything?
Even the best James Bond likes a
concession …

service for drinks and snacks and should the temperature need adjusting to shout out. He then said something I didn't quite hear and, rather loudly in the hushed auditorium, I asked Kristina, 'What was that?'

'He said, "And now please enjoy *SPECTRE* with the second best James Bond."'

'Well, who's the first?' I asked, just as the lights went down.

'*You* of course, my darling,' Kristina replied. '*You* are the best James Bond!'

'Oh yes!' I chuckled.

Our near neighbours obviously hadn't twigged it was me in the darkness, and must have thought it a very odd conversation going on between an aged man and his younger Swedish wife.

ON FINAL
REFLECTION

Still hanging on after all these years has made me realize and appreciate all the good luck, the fun, great fortune and the major milestones I've been a part of, both professionally and personally. I'm very grateful and have realized that if we look beyond the stereotypes, ageing, just like the rest of life, is a mixture of gains and losses. Though perhaps the greatest sadness in getting older means outliving loved ones, friends and colleagues. It's not easy to see your mates leave for the great cutting room in the sky, though admittedly I'm in no rush to join them, nor do I want to depress myself (or you) by listing all their names. Put it this way, watching the BAFTAs and the Academy Awards ceremonies becomes very sobering when they run the tape of 'those who have left us' each year. In fact, I'm in full agreement with Woody Allen when he said, 'Death – I'm strongly against it.'

Does mortality worry me? Yes, in all honesty, it does, as I think it does everyone. It's the unknown really, that's the worry. I'd certainly like to think that when my time comes I'll face it with all the dignity a coward can muster – and maybe with one last quick witticism.

When Bob Hope lay on his deathbed, aged 100, his wife Dolores raised the question of where he would like to be buried and in his last words, Bob replied: 'Surprise me.'

Though perhaps Alfred Hitchcock summed it up best, with his last words: 'One never knows the ending. One has to die to know exactly what happens after death, although Catholics have their hopes.'

I have my hopes too!

À bientôt …

AFTERWORD

I could not finish without saying something about a cause that is very close to my heart. I have been associated with UNICEF for over twenty-five years and in my humble opinion this wonderful organization has done so much to change the world, by improving the life of children.

I quote: 'The United Nations International Children's Emergency Fund is a United Nations programme headquartered in New York City that provides humanitarian and developmental assistance to children and mothers in developing countries.'

The organization is part of the UN but is not funded by the UN: support comes from individual countries, governments, corporations and individuals – hence the need for ambassadors like me to help raise awareness and funds. I won't say Kristina and I have visited all of the 190 countries and territories in which UNICEF has bases, but we have visited a significant number of them over the years.

I've said and written much about UNICEF over those years, but here I just really wanted to highlight how much more work there is still to do and the continuing importance of the charity. You see, over 20,000 children under the age of five die each day from preventable causes: I'm talking

about from illnesses like measles, malaria or tetanus; from marginalization, conflict and HIV/AIDS; from malnutrition and the lack of safe water and sanitation.

Children with these diseases and issues do not need to die and can be saved by vaccines, antibiotics, micronutrient supplementation, insecticide-treated bed nets and improved family care and breastfeeding practices.

I know I won't ever see the day when UNICEF is not needed but I do hope that day will come, and children do not die needlessly.

ACKNOWLEDGEMENTS

I'd like to extend my gratitude to Gareth Owen for taking my ramblings and notes and helping me to put this tome together.

My most appreciative thanks also to my terrific publishers, Michael O'Mara Books and their keen-eyed editor Louise Dixon, in our fourth happy collaboration, for all their help, encouragement and continued royalty cheques. The book's designer, Ana Bjezancevic, deserves a special mention for making the book, and me, look good. Iris Harwood helped proofread my jottings, so blame her if you spot any errors.

A big thanks also to Alan and Titti Tomkins, Katherine Dale and Andrew Boyle for answering the call of duty.

Last, but by no means least, reflecting back over all these years wouldn't be possible without the love and support of my wonderful family and my darling wife, Kristina.

The Tree of Love, sketched for my darling Kristina
on Valentine's Day 2017.